Don't Forget Your Cape!

What Preschoolers Teach Us About Leadership & Life

HUGH D. MACPHIE

authorHOUSE®

AuthorHouse™
1663 Liberty Drive
Bloomington, IN 47403
www.authorhouse.com
Phone: 1-800-839-8640

First published by AuthorHouse 11/17/2009

ISBN: 978-1-4490-4477-0 (e)
ISBN: 978-1-4490-4214-1 (sc)

Library of Congress Control Number: 2009911600

Printed in the United States of America
Bloomington, Indiana

This book is printed on acid-free paper.

Preschoolers believe that they can do anything.
And so should you.

Introduction

I have two kids, Jackson and John. As I write this, Jackson is six years old and John is four. In these first few years, the amount of information that children learn is almost unfathomable.

They learn to eat. Walk. Talk. Interact with others. And they start to figure out, in a very rudimentary way, the social rules and norms that shape how our society works.

In watching Jackson and John learn new things, *I've* learned as well. In fact, Jackson and John have taught me more than I could have imagined – about leadership, about working with others, and about life.

The things they've taught me aren't necessarily new or revolutionary. Many of the ideas they've helped me understand more clearly have been around for tens, or hundreds, or even thousands of years.

But they've helped me understand important ideas with greater precision – by simplifying theoretical concepts that are often made too complicated, and by reminding me about the immense potential that we all have.

Because preschoolers believe that they can do anything. And so should you.

Modern management theory tends to overcomplicate things. Too many management theorists have never seen a PowerPoint slide, or a complex graphic, or an acronym that they didn't like. Don't get me wrong: I *love* management theory. Yet I've always found that much of it is complex and difficult to understand … for the sake of being complex and difficult to understand.

It doesn't have to be this way.

The ideas and concepts my colleagues and I use in our consulting work every day are exceptionally valuable and powerful – but ultimately, many of these ideas and concepts can be distilled down into clear, simple axioms.

Making theories and concepts *difficult* to understand is easy. Making them *simple* – and distilling them to their core essence in a way that's easy for most people to understand – is *hard*. That's what I've tried to do here, with a bit of help from Jackson, John, and their pals.

When some of the great management theories and philosophical concepts are simplified, they become so much easier to execute and make real. I want to people *understand* big ideas. When they do, their potential to improve people's lives – inside and outside of the workplace – is exciting.

So what are just some of the big lessons that preschoolers teach us about leadership and life?

With preschoolers' unquestioned belief in their unlimited potential, what is the wisdom they would share?

Be a Superhero. Preschoolers believe in superheroes. And they are right. There are people we see every day doing the extraordinary in all walks of life. And each of us has the potential to make an incredible difference in the lives of others.

Don't Be Afraid to Fail. Preschoolers fail at things all the time. That's how they learn, grow, and become successful. We can learn from this. We should try to *avoid* failure, but never *fear* it.

Play Games. Make work fun – and do everything you can to keep score. Your own productivity, and that of the people around you, will improve.

Ask "Why?" Preschoolers ask "why?" And they ask it a lot. We should all ask probing questions to get at the underlying problems or opportunities that we face – not just the surface ones.

Be Creative. One idea plus another unrelated idea equals a new idea. That's creativity. It's that simple. Kids don't differentiate between creative jobs and non-creative jobs, and neither should we.

Take Smart Risks. Little kids take a lot of risks – some smart, some not so much! There isn't enough *smart* risk-taking going on in today's organizations. And only when people take smart risks can organizations grow and improve.

Pursue Your Passion. Achieve your optimum potential. Help others to do the same. And believe in your hunches. They usually tell the truth.

Celebrate Achievement. Kids celebrate even the smallest wins. Celebrating reminds us of the greatness in others – and in ourselves.

Get the Most Out of Every Single Day. Be a superhero. Leave your mark. Find your passion by working to change the world for the better – in small ways, and in bigger ones – every single day.

The preschoolers have got it right. *Anyone* can be a superhero: students, young professionals, teachers, small-business people, group managers, parents, team members, CEOs. Anyone who wants to make a positive difference, *can*. You just need to believe again – rekindling a passionate belief in yourself and your ability to make a profound and meaningful difference in the lives of those around you.

So this is a call to excellence. It is an invitation to remember a time when you believed that you could be a superhero, and to believe that you still can.

Be a Superhero

First, it was toy cars. Then Mighty Machines – like bull-dozers and excavators. Then dinosaurs.

And when our youngest son John was about three, he suddenly became passionately interested in something that, to him, was new and exciting: superheroes.

Soon after John's interest in superheroes began, my wife Michelle and I got him a small gift – that most *de rigueur* of superhero accessories: a cape.

Let me describe – in detail – the cape we got for John.

It's cheap. It probably cost about $6, taxes included. It is purple, with black trim. On the back is a gold circle, with a silver lightning bolt going through it on either side. There is Velcro around the neckpiece to hold the cape on tightly, but without risk of injury.

Truth is, it's a pretty tacky, low-cost costume accessory that you could probably find at any Walmart or Toys 'R' Us.

But to John, it was so much more than a cheap, purple piece of felt.

When he put on his cape, his back straightened. His eyes brightened. He walked with greater confidence. His language skills and pronunciation improved. And he was convinced – *convinced* – that there was no good deed that he could not accomplish.

He *became* a superhero.

Think about it. These are *physical, attitudinal,* and even *cognitive* changes. The symbolic catalyst for these changes may have been the cape, but what really mattered was John's belief in himself, who he was, and what he could do.

John started wearing his cape to preschool. And sure enough, in the week that followed, we started noticing *other* kids showing up with capes of their own.

Then they started wearing their Halloween costumes to preschool. Spider-Man. Superman. Iron Man. All of the Incredibles (who, if you know the story, wear costumes *sans* capes). And this was happening in the month of May, not October.

So for a short while, there were all these three-year-olds wearing capes, dressing up as superheroes, and protecting the world from evil.

There is an important lesson in all of this. Something we can learn from John and his preschool friends.

Too many people have *lost* their capes. Over time, they've lost their inner belief and conviction that they, too, can be superheroes.

Remember what superheroes believe – about themselves, their abilities, and the impact they can have.

They believe in doing the right thing, even when doing the right thing might not be popular.

They believe in standing up to those who hurt others.

And superheroes have *extreme confidence,* and fundamentally believe that they can achieve the extraordinary.

The World Needs More Superheroes

Preschool and kindergarten were a long time ago for most of us. And as people grow older, it is remarkable how they settle into a presupposed self-image. People get labeled. The numbers girl. The creative guy. The communications expert. The tough person to work with.

Those labels become self-perpetuating and start to harden like concrete.

I've noticed that the way people project themselves to others, often doesn't reflect who they truly are. But rather, people try to reflect *how they think others in society expect them to be.*

If you define yourself a certain way, that's who you become. I've seen that constraint lead too many people to feel limited, confined, and stuck. They start to convince themselves that maybe they aren't that great after all. They conclude that maybe they can't be a great songwriter. Or become a doctor. Or stand up to their mean and inappropriate co-worker. Or be a terrific parent.

Preschoolers believe that they can do anything. And so should you.

The good news is this. Superheroes *do* exist.

There are superheroes everywhere among us.

And I don't just mean the world-renowned heart surgeon who pioneered valve repair, or the business visionary who built the world's greatest travel adventure company, or the rock star who dedicated his energy to addressing the AIDS crisis in Africa.

I mean people that we see every day.

Like the neighbor who always shovels the snow or cuts the grass for the elderly couple who live next door – without asking for anything in return.

Or the nurse who works extra time at the end of each shift, without getting any additional pay, because her replacement has to drop his children off at the child care center.

Or the administrative assistant who never expects praise, never complains, and just quietly keeps the entire organization running smoothly because of her quiet, confident brilliance.

These are superheroes. Superheroes we see on the bus, or in line at the grocery store, or in the cubicle down the hall from where we work.

One of my favorite quotes is often attributed to a speech given by Nelson Mandela. It makes sense that it would be linked to Mandela, because the quote is worthy of one who worked calmly, but diligently and relentlessly, to change the world. But the actual source is from a book called "Return to Love" by Marianne Williamson.

She wrote: *"Our deepest fear is not that we are inadequate. Our deepest fear is that we are powerful beyond measure."*

Each of us – in our own unique ways – can be *powerful beyond measure.*

This is inspirational. It is an urgent message that needs to be shared. It is a reminder to each of us of our immense potential to achieve the extraordinary.

I see too many people holding back, for fear of offending others. Or ruffling feathers. Or being seen as a show-off. This timidity not only holds individuals back from personal success – it also holds back *our society as a whole* from achieving its full potential.

Don't Forget Your Cape

So this is a rejection of mediocrity, and an invitation to excellence.

Don't be afraid to be powerful beyond measure.

Make a massive difference in your own life, and in the lives of those around you.

Help others rise up to greatness by being great yourself.

Remember that preschoolers believe they can do anything. So should you.

Don't forget your cape. Be a superhero. And deliver on the promise of who you could become.

You will not only lead a happier, more productive life, but you will help create a better world.

Don't be Afraid to Fail

Think about the amount of change you went through between the time you were born and the time you started kindergarten. Think about how much you had to learn in a very short period of time.

You're born. You learn to recognize things. You learn to turn over, crawl, walk. You learn to eat solid food. You learn to recognize speech patterns and then try to replicate them. You learn to interact with others, recognize people who are nice and people who aren't. You have your first day at school, surrounded by many loud and new people in a large, foreign environment.

It is a difficult time of constant change, learning, and failure. But you did it. You not only survived, but you thrived.

Each of us failed every single day in our first five years of life. No one succeeds at eating, walking, or talking on the first try.

But a key difference between then and now, is that back in preschool, we didn't worry so much about what other people thought. We just tried new things, failed at them at first, learned from the experience, got better at them, and then eventually achieved success.

I remember when Jackson was learning to walk. He'd crawl over to a small coffee table or couch and climb up so that he could stand. Then, with a look of great determination, he'd use his hands and arms to move himself along and take small steps. Inch by inch, he'd move a bit forward.

He would smile with pride with each incremental inch that he moved ahead. He could tell he was on to something and that he was making progress. Then he'd fall. And sometimes cry.

But then he'd maneuver his way back, climb back up, and start the process over again.

Again, and again, and again.

When kids are learning to walk, there are no shortcuts. There is no easy way out. It is a tiresome, plodding, frustrating process of change and frequent failure. Just like many things that are important and worthwhile in life.

Failure is a Key to Success

I work with too many organizations where I see a tremendous fear of failure. Sometimes this is by design. But more often than not, it is an unintended consequence of management styles that don't welcome risk-taking, and of cultures that punish even the smallest misstep.

This rampant fear of failure is bad on three levels.

First, it prevents people from growing and learning by making mistakes – the way Jackson did as he was learning to walk.

Second, it holds organizations back, because new product ideas, or process innovations, or creative ways of serving customers more effectively never see the light of day. Why? Because people become too afraid to share their ideas in the first place.

And third, it holds national economies back, because with all those organizations and individuals so afraid to fail, innovation rates are reduced, and economic competitiveness suffers.

Throughout history, human progress and the growth of civilization have been a function of people and organizations *trying* things. Sometimes they work, and sometimes they don't.

17

If organizations don't fail every now and again, they're not trying hard enough. And if they have a culture that discourages the sharing of fresh thinking, new ideas, or creativity, then they are in trouble.

Because someone else will come along to eat their lunch.

I'm not saying that you should *try* to fail. But I am saying that you should *try*. Try process improvements, new products, new approaches, new ideas, and different ways of solving your customers' problems.

And don't be *afraid* to fail when you do.

Countless people who we consider visionaries, leaders, and tremendous successes didn't always start out that way. They learned through failure too.

- J.K. Rowling's first Harry Potter book was initially rejected by a dozen publishing houses.

- Michael Jordan was cut from his high school basketball team.

- Walt Disney was fired from his job at a newspaper for "lacking imagination".

Each of these people knew they had talent, followed their passions, took smart risks, and made a difference in the world.

Feeling Comfortable? Chances Are, You're Not Growing and Learning.

Only by getting outside of our comfort zones – as individuals and as organizations – do we grow and improve. One-year-olds aren't satisfied with crawling as their only means of getting around, so they try walking. And eventually, they learn to walk.

But keep in mind how many times you failed before mastering the art of walking. Remember this, the next time you feel anxious about taking on an exciting new role, or project, or activity that might be outside your comfort zone.

Don't be afraid of failure – even when people are looking at you. *Get* outside your comfort zone. Take on new and different challenges enthusiastically.

You will increase your chances of success, you will learn new skills and gain fresh perspective that only comes from experience.

And you might just have fun along the way.

Just like Jackson did when he took those first few steps.

Have a Vision and Communicate it Relentlessly

One of my favorite pieces of home video shows Jackson coming into his room and seeing his new "big bed" for the first time. He was ready to graduate from sleeping in a crib to sleeping in a bed, and we decided to capture his first reaction to his new bed on video.

Here's what happened: Jackson gets to the top of the stairs, then waddles into his bedroom, and he starts to smile. Then his eyes brighten up, and he starts to sprint (as best he can at that age) to tackle the new bed.

He just *tackles* it.

Then he lifts himself up on the side of the bed, climbs up onto it, and says, "WOW – big bed!" Then he goes nuts. He gives the bed a huge hug, grabs the pillows, and starts jumping around on the Winnie the Pooh bedspread. Then he sits down – looking elated, saying "Wow!" a few more times – and gives Winnie the Pooh three high-fives.

So why did Jackson react like he had just won the lottery? For him, the big bed was *symbolic*. It was a rite of passage. The bed wasn't just a change in where he would sleep. It was a step up to a new level. He *knew* that it was, because Michelle and I *primed* him for it. We talked to him about it in advance, and even got his help in choosing the Winnie the Pooh bedspread.

We communicated the vision, positioned it as exciting and a new level of responsibility. We said to him – over and over again – that moving to a big bed was *exciting*. And we involved him in the process, by getting his input on the choice of bedsheets.

Let's keep in mind: absent *positioning* the move to a big bed as a good thing, it could have resulted in *tears*.

The crib – with its nice musical mobile, comfort, familiarity, and protective bars, was *gone*. It was replaced by a much bigger, different sleeping place. The bigger bed was something you could fall out of very easily and hurt yourself. It was foreign, massive, and came with a potential risk of injury.

Jackson had a happy reaction to this significant change because we took the time to engage him in advance, and communicated a vision to him consistently and frequently.

Because most people *really* don't like change. And in today's world, organizations are going through change processes *all the time.*

It used to be that organizations would go through change initiatives that would be linked to a major project (like putting in a new computer system or going through a merger). There was a "change era" – and then it was all over.

Often, once the "change era" ended, those who disliked the change would breathe a huge sigh of relief and hope that things would just go back to the way they were before. Old ways of doing things – and old work patterns – die hard. Especially with people who were perfectly comfortable and okay with the way things used to be.

In today's organizations, while discrete change initiatives still exist, the "change era" is *never* over. Successful organizations are constantly in the process of re-inventing themselves, and structuring themselves to be successful into the future.

Major change initiatives have been the subject of much study and research. And in general, the track record of these efforts is very poor. In a study examining organizational change programs, PricewaterhouseCoopers estimated that nearly 75 percent of all major change programs fail.

A big reason for these expensive failures is that leaders didn't adequately *tell the story* of why change was happening. They didn't adequately engage their teams in planning for change, sharing and involving them in their vision of how the organization would be stronger at the end of the transformation process.

People prefer what they are used to, because what they are used to is *comfortable*.

Remember Frasier Crane's father Marty from the TV show *Frasier*? Remember Marty's living-room chair? As a well-paid psychiatrist, Frasier could have afforded to buy his father any chair he wanted. But Marty didn't want change. He wanted the old, plaid chair with the duct tape on the arms, because it was the one he was used to and it was comfortable.

People resist and dislike change for good reasons. They want predictability and a sense of control over their day-to-day lives. People become *good* at what they do, even if what they do (and the way they do it) is no longer useful to their organization. So for many people, the natural tendency is to dislike and *work against* new ideas or different ways of doing things.

One of the most important roles any leader has, helping people to understand the benefits of change and the reasons why change is happening. That doesn't mean that everyone is going to *like* the reasons. Or that they are going to automatically accept them. But people crave logic. A *rationale*. They want the knowledge that there is a plan, and that change is happening based on a good reason or justification.

Sometimes that's easy; sometimes it can be more challenging. But effective leaders develop a *narrative*. They find a logical story that they *personally* believe, that describes how excited they are about the future of their organization. Leaders share the story in a way that each individual can personally relate to, helping them to understand how they can be involved, and shape change. And leaders relentlessly and consistently share that narrative with their team.

But let me be clear. As a leader, you have to *believe* your own vision. You need to intellectually and emotionally *buy into* the change narrative that you are communicating.

If leaders don't believe in the change they are trying to communicate, their team members will know it. The same is true of toddlers. Two-year-olds can tell immediately if you're not confident in what you're saying. If your words, your facial expressions, and your body language are not aligned, preschoolers get a mixed message. And they become reluctant to do what you're asking them.

That mixed message, when the words don't match the speaker's tone, is called *narrative incongruence* – when one part of the message you're conveying doesn't match with another. People get very tense and uncomfortable when they feel narrative incongruence – regardless if they are a two-year-old or an employee. Worse, that mixed message erodes the trust they have in their leaders, or in their parents.

Enthusiasm Doesn't Happen on Its Own; You Need to Build It

So how do you get people excited and enthusiastic about change? By *being* excited and enthusiastic about change, and building *change momentum* within your organization.

When I was in preschool, my family moved to California for a year. For a five-year-old, this could have been a scary, difficult, gut-wrenching change – leaving home, friends, and familiarity.

But that wasn't how my parents positioned it.

Whenever they spoke of our move to California, they did it with excitement and enthusiasm. Their tone of voice was positive and upbeat. They talked about Disneyland and the ocean. And my parents told me the best news that a five-year-old boy growing up in the late 1970s could possibly hear: that they sold *Star Wars* action figures in California too! Just like back home.

My parents had a narrative. We were going on a one-year sabbatical for my dad's work. We would live in a comfortable house in San Carlos. I would go to kindergarten there and meet new friends.

I understood the logic behind why we were doing this, and had comfort from the fact that the details were under control.

But they also had genuine enthusiasm for the move and conveyed that enthusiasm consistently. Their words, their tone, and the look in their eyes told me that it was going to be a great experience. So I felt excited about it as well.

I felt that living in California was going to be cool. And my conclusions about this new change were drawn entirely from the way my parents positioned it. To this day, some of my fondest memories are from the time I spent there.

Here's a Formula:
Use Logos and Pathos

Is communicating a vision for change easy? Not always. But there is a quick formula that can help, and it is a formula that has been around for thousands of years.

The ancient Greeks were very serious about the study of *rhetoric.* They were masters in the use of what they called *logos* and *pathos* to construct arguments and win over audiences. *Logos* is the use of logical reasoning to construct an argument through facts, statistics, and objectivity.

We see logos used all the time. For instance, when marketers claim that their product is *37 percent more effective than the competition,* and back up their claim with a reason to believe it, they are making a logical appeal.

Pathos is about emotional appeals. It tugs at the heartstrings, thereby getting people to like something on a gut level by evoking strong emotions.

When our son Jackson was moving to the "big bed," we used logos: he was getting bigger, he needed more space, and he was ready for it. And we also used pathos: it was going to be exciting.

Jesse Jackson's Powerful Use of Pathos

Few people have ever made such impressive use of pathos as the Reverend Jesse Jackson in his famous "Keep Hope Alive" speech, delivered to the Democratic National Convention in 1988.

Jesse Jackson's rhetoric soars in this speech.

In one section, he reminds the audience of his humble upbringing, born to a teenage mother who used to go to work early. His mother who, on Thanksgiving, had to prepare *another* family's turkey first, and then bring home the leftovers around eight o'clock at night for Jesse and his family. That was when they had *their* dinner.

This was a brilliant narrative, designed to create sympathy and communicate to people that Jesse Jackson was a symbol of how they, too, could rise from humble beginnings and make a difference.

This pure emotional storytelling crescendos to one of the great lines of the speech: "I was born in the slum, but the slum was not born in me. And it wasn't born in you, and you can make it!"

And the crowd goes wild! They loved it.

Jesse Jackson was showing that he shared the challenges and values of so many who *had* struggled, or who *were* struggling, to achieve their dreams and live a better life. So he was appealing to *everybody.* Because *everyone* believes that they have had struggles and challenges, and that they are working to achieve a better life.

So the formula for developing a vision for change includes both *logos* – a logical appeal that articulates why change is necessary – and *pathos,* which helps people to be emotionally engaged and excited.

To create a truly compelling vision or narrative, you need *both*.

It isn't enough to just present a logical, intellectually clear rationale as to why major change is good. You also have to show that change will help achieve shared goals, that it will reinforce shared values, and that it is the *right* thing to do.

But Change is Still Hard

Harvard Business School's John Kotter is a world-renowned change-management expert who has written extensively on approaches to successfully deliver change within organizations. In his book, *Leading Change,* Kotter lists eight steps that organizations, large and small, should follow in helping employees accept and embrace new ways of doing things.

Little did Michelle and I know that we were applying change-management theory with Jackson when he made the move to the big bed! As it turns out, Michelle and I were applying Kotter's fourth principle – Communicate the Vision.

And you can't just communicate your vision for change once, and check it off of your to-do list. Circulating one interoffice memo, sending out a blast e-mail, or calling a single staff meeting isn't enough. Communicating and articulating a vision for the future takes time, repetition, and an ongoing commitment from leaders.

Be Part of the Solution

Being enthusiastic about change isn't solely the responsibility of the leadership in any organization. I've seen many cases where that leadership simply wasn't there;

where the concepts of sharing a vision and repeating it enthusiastically simply weren't things that managers did.

But that doesn't let any of us off the hook.

Even in the absence of a clear vision from above, or without enthusiastic, repetitive communication of the benefits of change, we need to generate *our own* enthusiasm. By being part of the solution, and getting enthusiastically behind change within our organizations.

All of us, as individuals, have a choice. Every single day.

We can go about our tasks, our work, our professions, and our lives with the attitude that they are dull or uninteresting. (And unfortunately, that's what many people do – either consciously or subconsciously.)

Or we can decide to be enthusiastic and excited about our work, and make the most out of every situation.

Jackson slept very well the night he moved to his big bed. Maybe it was because he was a tired toddler who had had a long day. But it may also have been, at least in part, because he had decided that this new change was going to be a good thing for him, and an important step forward.

See the *opportunity* in any change or in any new situation. Make the most of it. And chances are, you'll sleep better at night as well.

Play Games

My kids don't like getting dressed in the morning. They quite prefer hanging out in their pajamas and playing. They see getting dressed as a boring chore, one they would rather just avoid.

But they *do* like playing catch. And they're at an age where they can catch things pretty well. So I created a game. It's called: "who wants to catch their clothes?"

It's really simple.

I toss clothing items from the top of the staircase down to where Jackson or John stand ready to catch them. I usually start with a shirt, then pants, and finally socks (which are smallest, but most ball-like when rolled up, and therefore fairly easy to catch). That way, we usually end on a high note.

Once they've caught their clothes (or bobbled them, as the case may be) they are usually ready to get dressed.

It's all in how the task is positioned.

If I say "get dressed," it feels like a chore that takes them away from something fun. If I say "who wants to catch their clothes?" there they are standing at the bottom of the staircase, knees bent, hands up and at the ready, looking like short versions of baseball or cricket players.

One approach is a chore, the other is a game.

It's About Motivation

People get more done, do things better, and are less likely to want to quit their jobs if they are motivated and having fun.

If they're *not* motivated and having fun, they aren't as productive, make more mistakes, and are probably out looking for another job.

Business literature is replete with theories and studies on motivating employees. But from my perspective, it basically comes down to three things:

1. Help people find a way to get passionate about what they do;

2. Make the work you do engaging and fun; and

3. Keep score.

We've already talked about having a vision and communicating it relentlessly. That goes a long way toward helping people find a way to get passionate about what they do. So this chapter is about having fun at work, and finding ways to keep score.

Make Work Fun

I am a very big believer that corporate culture can be a source of sustainable competitive advantage for organizations. That means the *vibe and energy* of an organization can help it to be more successful, over time, than its competitors.

This is especially true for service-oriented organizations that place customer service at the very top of their list of priorities and values.

I don't eat fast food very much. But my favorite fast-food restaurant chain is called Lick's.

Lick's Homeburgers and Ice Cream is essentially a burgers-and-fries operation, competing against McDonald's, Burger King, Wendy's, and others. But when you walk into a Lick's, you notice that a few things are different.

First, there's often a long line. That's because they make really good hamburgers, and have a fantastic secret sauce called "Guk" that they put on their burgers. That long line moves quickly, because they've got systems in place to move people through.

The second thing you notice is that the employees aren't acting in the way we've come to expect at a fast-food restaurant. They are *singing*. The teenagers who are flipping hamburgers, making fries, getting drinks, and taking orders, are periodically *breaking out into song*. One person usually takes the lead, and then five or six others respond – chanting or singing in unison.

For both the staff and the customers, it feels a lot more like summer camp than waiting in line for fast food. *Everyone* is having a good time.

This is because Lick's saw an opportunity. Yes, you need a great product. But rather than investing in expensive advertising, why not invest in training people really, really well, and purposefully creating an atmosphere that's fun?

That's exactly what they've done.

Lick's works hard on building enthusiasm, and improving the self-confidence of their staff members. And in the long run, they *save* money by not needing to spend as much time and money attracting and hiring new people – because the people they have are having so much fun at work.

Keeping Score

Having fun and creating an energetic atmosphere can go a long way toward helping your organization to succeed. But so does keeping score.

Jackson plays video games. And without wanting to sound like a curmudgeon, I've had great difficulty understanding the appeal of some of them. For example, there's this game called Mario Party, which Jackson and his friends really, really like to play.

So I decided to try to deconstruct what was going on, and understand why these kids love this game so much. In Mario Party, they lead their characters through all kinds of races, games, and activities. Depending on how well they do, they earn points. Once they accumulate enough points, they can buy things. Not real things, but things within the video game, using the points they have.

To me, the races, games, and activities themselves don't look all that exciting. But what seems to really motivate Jackson and his pals are those *points.* Let me emphasize this: the points and the things they can buy with them are all *within* the game; they can't transfer their points to get a coupon to buy something real.

It is point accumulation for the sake of point accumulation.

Just ask any of the millions of people (most of whom who are adults) who play video games: it is remarkable how motivating electronic scorekeeping can be.

There is huge potential to apply this same principle – that of keeping score – to *all kinds* of work- or volunteer-related circumstances. Computer software and online tracking make scorekeeping easier and more immediate than in the past. People can check out how many points they have – and how they're stacking up against others – in real time.

The Barack Obama campaign used online scorekeeping to motivate their volunteers during the 2008 U.S. presidential election.

Through *www.my.barackobama.com* volunteers could log in and see how well they were doing by clicking on their own personalized dashboard. Volunteers earned points based on the potential impact of their activities. For example, a volunteer who made a phone call encouraging someone to support the campaign was awarded three points. Someone who hosted a pro-Obama event was awarded fifteen points.

Each volunteer's dashboard clearly displayed how many points he or she had accumulated, and allowed them to compare their point totals with other Obama activists.

The point system created a sense of *competition* among Obama supporters. It created an incentive for people to do more and work harder – much like Jackson's video game.

It is remarkable, above and beyond financial incentives, how these mini-competitions can motivate people. Because they just want to win for the pure pleasure of winning.

It comes back to the old adage that what gets measured gets done.

But *choosing* what to measure is key. Organizations have to think long and hard about *what* to measure, and *how* to keep score. The place to start is your organization's overall mission, vision, and objectives. Measure those things that contribute *the most* to your overall mission, vision, and objectives, and you'll be on the right track.

This is what key performance indicators – or KPIs – are all about: measuring things that are most important to your overall success, and then tracking how well each person is contributing.

Choosing what to measure through key performance indicators is hard. Even when you think you've designed a points system that will motivate people to do the right things, the law of unintended consequences can rear its ugly head.

Like it did in my eighth-grade shop class.

Our shop teacher had a neat system whereby you got points for completing different tasks or projects. So I got a certain number of points for the horrifically ugly candle holder that I made, which my parents are good enough to still display in their home. Based on the points system, my classmates and I got a different number of points if we made a wooden table, or plastic keychain, or some other household object.

But part of our shop class curriculum was also *drafting:* making technical drawings of how things were supposed to be built. Most of us hated drafting – which was still done using paper and pencil at the time – except one kid: Martin Wainwright.

Martin was the smartest kid in the class. And he had figured something out: you got more points for drafting, per hour of effort, than for making things from plastic or wood.

So every shop class, Martin would just sit down and do drafting. And he got an A+. Not because he was the most skilled person when it came to shop class as a whole, but because he had figured out a way to beat the system.

This is the law of unintended consequences at its very best. The points system had been designed to encourage people to be productive and learn a variety of shop-related skills. But instead, here was someone getting a great mark for churning out drafting drawings, not for the broader learning that was intended.

Provide the Right Incentive, and People Find Ways of Getting Things Done

The idea here is to motivate people in ways that encourage them to spend their time and talents optimally – in ways that deliver the most for your organization.

KPIs are useful for complex organizations that seek to compete and win over time. But the principle of providing an incentive that gets work done isn't complicated, and can be applied to more straightforward goals.

Like getting some new artwork for your refrigerator.

One of my colleagues, Karin Schnarr, is one of Jackson's and John's favorite people. Karin understands the importance of providing the right incentive to achieve a desired outcome. One time after returning home from vacation, Karin stopped by our place with gifts for the kids. Karin stepped through the front door, gifts in hand, and was greeted by John asking, "Karin, did you get me a present?!"

Indeed she had. For both of them.

But not so fast.

Jackson and John were going to have to *work* for their presents. So Karin said, "I will give you your presents. But only after you have drawn me a picture!"

Without hesitation, they were off.

They searched urgently for crayons and paper, and then sat down and worked away.

A few minutes later, they returned, their *oeuvres* complete, ready for presentation. For all their hard work, Jackson and John had earned their gifts. And Karin received original artwork to decorate her refrigerator door.

The point is this: Jackson and John didn't fight the task. And they figured out how to do it on their own. They didn't ask their mom or me to get paper and crayons, find them a place to work, and make suggestions about what they might consider drawing. They just got on with it, gathering everything they needed with minimal help or supervision.

Why? They had an incentive. They were motivated. They found the resources they needed on their own. And they got the job done.

Play Games and Everybody Wins

By motivating people within your organization, you can improve productivity, help people have more fun, and increase retention of the people who are really good at their jobs. And the truth is, people who may *not* be a good fit for your organization, or who are simply in the wrong job, might not like the scorekeeping.

No one likes getting low scores compared to their peers. But ultimately, it is in *those individuals'* best interest to identify ways of improving their performance, or to find work that more closely matches their skill set.

Find ways of making your work environment more fun and engaging – regardless of what it is you do. And keep score – focusing on the key factors that are most important to the achievement of your organization's mission, vision, and key objectives.

You will have more motivated people – focusing on things that matter and delivering better results over time.

Ask "Why?"

When John was three years old, he started asking a very important question: "Why?"

Three-year-olds don't just ask "why?" once and then let the issue drop. They ask it repeatedly, probingly, often laddering down to a point where you can no longer answer their question. At that point, the conversation usually goes something like this:

Three-year-old: "Why?"

Parent: "Well, because."

Like most three-year-olds, John was genuinely trying to figure things out. This questioning is an important part of a child's developmental process. Young children use what Swiss psychologist Jean Piaget called *primitive reasoning*. Kids start seeking a logic and rationale for everything – from why the sky is blue to why they have to go to bed earlier than they want to. They want to know why things are the way they are. So they ask a lot of questions.

The three-year-olds have got it right.

Seeking the root causes of a problem, or probing deeply into the reason why something is, can be enlightening. Asking "why?" – again, and again, and again – can help expose the real issue as opposed to the surface one. It can yield startling insights. It can help uncover the truth, or bring precision to the real objective that needs to be achieved.

We can learn from this. And some organizations have.

The Five "Whys"

Asking "why" until you uncover the root cause of a problem is actually a sophisticated management tool. Sakichi Toyoda, the founder of Toyota, developed the concept of the Five Whys. This concept is not all that different from John continually asking "why?"

Toyoda believed that asking "why" up to, say, five times, helps strip away extraneous information until only the core essence of the problem remains. Then, once the real problem is identified, better solutions can be developed.

Using the Five Whys and then making improvements based on a better understanding of the true nature of a problem is the foundation of the *Kaizen* system used by Toyota. *Kaizen* is the Japanese word for "improvement." At Toyota, they have a philosophy of improving continuously. They make small changes, see if those changes work, and then continue to adjust. While the changes may be small, this *philosophy* adds up to large, system-wide, continuous improvements.

All Toyota employees – from the CEO to the summer intern – are expected to find ways of doing things better, with greater quality and more efficiency, *every single day*. When that happens across a large organization, a *culture* of continuous improvement is created. *Kaizen* has become ingrained into Toyota's corporate culture and has become a source of competitive advantage.

People within today's organizations don't ask "why?" nearly enough. Nor do they question decisions that have already been made, for fear of embarrassing higher-ups or having to write off sunk costs. Some don't feel like they can question projects or initiatives, for fear of retribution or because someone might tell them that "isn't their role."

This is nonsense. I would encourage *everyone* to always ask smart questions – even if that might mean taking a risk. Think about the consequences of *not* asking the smart questions.

I would like to have seen people asking "why?" more often in a number of situations where significant problems could have been avoided, or at the very least reduced.

Like within the old Pontiac division of General Motors.

I wonder if anyone ever asked, "Why do we think the Pontiac Aztek is going to be successful?"

From my perspective, the Aztek was one ugly vehicle. And I can't put my finger on the target audience that would *cheer* for it, love it, and be proud to own it. During the Aztek's five-year production run, only 115,000 were made. By automotive industry standards, this was not good. By comparison, in the year 2006, more than 387,000 Toyota Corollas were sold in the United States alone.

In my view, if the employees at Pontiac had asked "why" a bit more, they might have redesigned the Aztek to be more in line with consumer tastes, or abandoned the project before millions more had been sunk into it.

New Coke

It actually tasted better.

After spending millions of dollars on strategic planning, market research, and advertising, the Coca-Cola Company developed and launched New Coke in April of 1985. They had developed a new, sweeter formula that consumers preferred in taste tests over the existing Coca-Cola recipe. But New Coke was met with intense backlash soon after its launch.

Loyal Coke drinkers felt *betrayed*.

For the Coca-Cola Company, New Coke was a marketing and public relations nightmare. The only good news for Coca-Cola executives was that consumers began stocking up cases of the *old* Coke, in advance of its pending discontinuation!

Of course, that discontinuation never really happened. At least not for long. Coca-Cola Classic, which used the old Coke recipe, was launched within seventy-nine days of New Coke's introduction. The rollout of New Coke created one of the most fascinating studies in consumer behavior of all time, and fodder for much analysis and second-guessing.

Much has been written about the New Coke case study. Sergio Zyman, who was chief marketing officer at Coca-Cola, even offers his perspective in an excellent book called *The End of Marketing as We Know It*.

Maximizing the upside and minimizing the downside of business decisions means asking those fundamental, basic questions. I wonder if someone ever asked, "Even if New Coke does taste better and tests well across all of our consumer segments, *why* do we think die-hard Coke drinkers, who love us as a symbol of authenticity and tradition, won't react badly to the *idea* of New Coke?"

In my view, Coca-Cola is a brand that profoundly symbolizes sameness and Santa Claus and warm, dusty summer afternoons. The concept of a *new* Coke is antithetical to all of the symbolism and meaning of the Coca-Cola brand. The attribute "new" was, is, and forever shall be incongruous with what Coca-Cola is all about.

Ask Stupid Questions. They Rock.

There are few moments in meetings with clients that I relish more than this. There we all are, gathered around a big boardroom table, when suddenly a more junior person somewhat coyly, but with conviction, begins to say: "I know that this might sound like a stupid question, but …"

Now they have my attention. Something insightful is about to happen. Because chances are, that young staffer is going to challenge a presumed assumption, or question an objective, or challenge a sacred cow, or bring a subconscious issue that everybody knows about and put it right onto the table for everyone to see, whether they like it or not.

By asking that stupid question, they are about to call out – preferably indirectly and with a subtlety lost on the older and more jaded – the elephant that stands boldly in the living room. Or put differently, the *real* issue that everyone else is skirting around because of its awkwardness or political ramifications.

I love moments like that. They provide clarity, fresh thinking, and an appropriate digression from the anticipated arc of the conversation. Then we can usually identify more profound, difficult, and (more often than not) personality-oriented issues that truly need to be discussed before more fundamental progress can be made.

And usually when someone says, "I know that this might sound like a stupid question, but …" I unabashedly heap praise on the person who dared speak the truth. Because they asked "why". And that's how we make progress.

Ask "why". Ask it a lot. Make a point within your teams of encouraging the spirit of the "five whys."

Don't ask "why" to the point of paralysis or at the expense of seizing important opportunities. But to ensure that the right thinking has been done – especially at the beginning of any project or initiative. Because for very complex and all-too-human reasons, questioning the basic fundamentals of an initiative becomes much, much harder after it is already in progress.

I suspect that there probably came a time when some project leader or vice president's career was closely connected to the launch of the Pontiac Aztek. At that point, it becomes very, very difficult – after hundreds of millions have been invested – for any staff person to call into question the feasibility of the project.

At that point, it takes tremendous courage – and great skill – to tactfully question the sinking of further resources into a project that has a high emotional importance for senior leaders within any organization.

And at that point, the pendulum has sadly swung away from doing the right thing and over to preserving senior leaders' credibility and bonuses. This is a gross failure of too many modern organizations. I urge such leaders to know when the right thing to do is to kill a project, and I encourage the rest of us to politely, but pointedly and clearly, ask "why?"

Three-year-olds know a thing or two about figuring the world out. Let's learn from their example. Ask "why" to get to the root causes of problems and find more useful and insightful solutions.

In the long run, that's always the right thing to do.

Share

His technique resembled that of a three-legged crab.

When John was first learning to crawl, he developed a unique approach to getting around, which involved sticking one leg out and moving his other leg beneath himself. While he might not have earned many points for style, it worked. And within about a week, John got very good at crawling.

When they are learning to crawl, babies are on their own. They can't consult crawling manuals to learn the best techniques. And while babies can watch one another to try to figure out what works and what doesn't, they can't talk. So they can't share tips with one another or communicate best practices.

That's the big difference in the way that *organizations* can learn and improve compared to the way John learned to crawl: knowledge sharing. John didn't have to worry about communicating his progress or innovations to others, but organizations *do*.

Great things can happen, and organizations can become far more productive and successful, when people share. But people don't necessarily share things on their own. They need to be encouraged and rewarded for sharing.

Which is why I am a strong believer in using systems and incentives that encourage people to *share* their ideas and thinking, and to tell their co-workers about new and better ways of doing their work.

One of our clients, Patrick Nelson, is a huge believer in the critical importance of people within the workplace just *talking* to one another. His policy is that his team members need to go above and beyond when it comes to apprising one another about what they're up to. They share their thinking and proposed projects with people from *other* departments within his organization as well. Patrick wants his team to build a reputation of working with others and sharing information: providing project updates and sharing knowledge, information, and best practices with others. That way, there are no surprises, and ultimately, better results.

Now, if you've been to preschool lately, you know that toddlers don't always like to share.

Many a battle has been waged over a toy someone else wants, or who gets a turn on the beanbag chair, or who gets the *red* Hot Wheels car.

Let me tell you: these battles can be vicious.

I wish that I could say that similarly vicious battles didn't occur over scarce resources or information in business organizations.

But do they ever.

Information is power. And battles over information, and who gets to see it, are not uncommon.

Those who horde information are being as immature as a two-year-old not sharing his toy after his turn is over. And they are doing their shareholders, board of directors, or whomever else relies on their organization to deliver results, a tremendous disservice.

Developing a culture of information-sharing takes leadership and frequent reminders to others within your organization about the reasons why sharing is so important. People need to be reminded of the benefits that come from remembering and *working* to share, because sharing takes time. It can feel inefficient, and it can feel unnecessary.

Studies show that organizations that seek to capture knowledge, share it, and establish best practices and preferred ways of doing things are often more successful. The real opportunity is to create what's been called a *learning organization.*

Chris Argyris, a Harvard Business School professor, has developed an important body of work about building learning organizations. He has written extensively about the roadblocks and barriers that get in the way of organizations being able to learn, and about things that can be done to create more knowledge-sharing. If you really want to get into the concept of building a learning organization, his work is a good place to start.

But for now, here are some tips that we've developed over the years.

Simple Steps to Get People to Share Information and Develop Best Practices

There are a number of simple steps your organization can take immediately to share, learn, and ultimately improve results.

1. **Develop a *culture* in which people are encouraged to share.** Do like Patrick Nelson did, and try to gain a reputation as being someone who goes out of his or her way to share thinking, ideas, and project updates. Set up regular meetings to share ideas. Or better yet, tie best-practice sharing to performance evaluation.

2. **Conduct post-mortems, and distribute the best practices that emerge from them.** At the end of any project or initiative, do an honest assessment of what went well, what went poorly, and how you can do better next time. Unfortunately, post-mortems are the poor cousin of the project-management process. Too often, they get postponed, they don't get taken seriously, or they never happen at all. Make post-mortems – and the written reports covering steps on how you will continuously improve – a priority within your team and organization. That way, you can make best-practice sharing and continuous improvement a *program.* Then people will get into the habit of doing post-mortems and sharing the results.

3. **Reward people who share good ideas and process improvements.** This is especially important within competitive organizations where people might be inclined to keep good ideas to themselves. Reward people who share, and praise them publicly for doing so.

4. **Develop a "current best approach" that is regularly updated, and teach people how the "current best approach" works.** Having a document that people read doesn't cut it. Education and teaching are key parts of this process, especially when it means un-learning old, less-effective ways of doing things. Document the very best way your organization

does something, and constantly seek to make it even better.

Unlike infants who are learning to crawl, organizations *can* share tips and best ways of doing things. When he started crawling, John couldn't communicate his process improvements and learning to other babies.

But organizations can.

Talk. Share. And by so doing, your projects, your organization, and ultimately, your own career will be more successful.

Be Creative

Germs are evil.

One of the most significant reasons why patients within hospitals contract deadly infections, is because people don't wash their hands. More than just about any other precaution, hand-washing is encouraged by public health officials to reduce the risk of getting influenza or other superbugs. And in our household, we strongly encourage our kids to wash their hands so that everyone is more likely to stay healthy.

So in our house, we don't just have soap. We also have a hand-sanitizer dispenser.

And Jackson, who is often in a hurry to get back to playing with his LEGO or action figures, sometimes decides to forgo a thorough hand-washing, and just uses the hand sanitizer.

One time, when Jackson hurried out of the washroom to get back to what he was doing, we asked: "Did you wash your hands?!?"

And he said, "No – but I used hanitizer!"

Hanitizer?

Jackson had just invented a new word for hand-sanitizer. Someone should go and get a trademark for the word immediately. But for now, this is the word we use in our household for hand sanitizer because it is a *creative* new way of expressing an idea efficiently.

In today's business world, the idea of creativity is too often perceived as something that only people in advertising agencies or design houses do. Too often, we don't think of being creative as central to each of our jobs.

But it is.

Creativity Is Very Simple: One Existing Idea + Another Existing Idea = A New Idea

You can be creative – no matter what your job, role or situation happens to be.

One existing idea, plus another unrelated existing idea, equals a new idea. It's that simple.

Creativity is essential to the success of our own personal careers, and to the future of modern organizations.

In today's knowledge economy, there is a premium paid for workers who are part of what Dr. Richard Florida of the University of Toronto calls the *creative class:* people who drive innovation and creativity into the economy, and/or people who are knowledge-based workers.

This creative class is far larger than just graphic designers and people who write copy at advertising agencies. It includes people who come up with innovative ideas and fresh thinking that, when applied to products and services, have an impact.

Like creating colorful luggage.

The Heys Luggage Company recognized that the luggage on the market all tended to be black. Standing around any airport luggage carousel, you can see most passengers trying to determine exactly which black suitcase belongs to them. Many of us tie colored ribbons around our luggage, so we know which one is ours (which is *one* way of being creative).

Heys got creative in another way.

They created a line of colorful, lightweight luggage that sets them apart from the competition. Heys bags look different and cool, and they have built their business by challenging the preconceived notion that luggage had to be black.

Your Experiment Failed? That's Great News.

Thinking creatively is also about taking an idea or concept that failed at one thing and applying it to something different – where it can be hugely successful.

Spencer Silver had a problem: his glue didn't work. It was just a little bit sticky, but didn't actually hold things together the way most glues are supposed to. What the glue *could* do, was hold paper together temporarily without ripping it.

Silver presented his semi-sticky glue to his colleagues at the large company where he worked: 3M. He wasn't able to generate much interest. No one could think of a purpose for a glue that didn't work … until Arthur Fry, another 3M scientist, came along.

Arthur Fry had a problem too. He sang in his church choir and was frustrated at the way his makeshift bookmarks would fall out of his hymn book, interrupting his singing, causing him to lose his place.

Then Arthur Fry remembered learning about Spencer Silver's innovation that allowed two pieces of paper to be stuck together temporarily. When applied to his bookmarks, the semi-sticky glue would allow him to mark pages without the bookmark falling out or moving.

Fry presented his idea for a new product using the semi-sticky glue to the leaders at 3M. He thought that there might be a more widespread interest in this new way of marking pages.

Was there ever.

They had created the Post-It Note. Spencer Silver's temporary adhesive glue, plus Arthur Fry's need to mark the pages of his hymn book without ripping them, resulted in an innovation that has been wildly successful for 3M.

Many successful innovations and products are the result this kind of creative thinking: taking something that had been designed with one purpose in mind, and then finding a completely different purpose for it.

Pfizer, the pharmaceutical company, was working on a new heart and blood pressure medication. But over the course of their clinical trials, they kept hearing about a curious side effect that men taking their new drug were experiencing...

Viagra was originally being developed to help people with high blood pressure and cardiac problems. When Pfizer thought about the potential market for an erectile dysfunction drug, they turned their innovation into a much more substantial business opportunity.

Macro-Creativity

Developing a new drug category, inventing sticky notes, and changing the way people think about luggage are major innovations. This is what I call macro-creativity: using creativity and innovation in a way that transforms business markets or creates entirely new ones.

Harvard business professor Clayton M. Christensen has extensively studied what he calls *disruptive innovations.* These are innovations that change the game – often coming from smaller or new organizations within a business category.

These "game changers" often start small, focus on what appear to be unprofitable segments of the market, and whose offerings often cost a lot less than the existing market leaders' products and services. And they are often ignored by the bigger players, who write off what they see as small players whose innovations will likely go nowhere.

Until, of course, the game changers' products get better.

And then, before they know it, the organizations that used to dominate a market suddenly have a problem on their hands.

In the 1960s and '70s, the "Big Three" car manufacturers ruled the North American auto industry. And then, along came the low-cost Japanese car manufacturers who launched smaller, cheaper cars into the market. Over time, the quality and reputation of the Japanese cars rose dramatically – consistently eroding the market share and profitability of the "Big Three."

Another example of a disruptive innovation: digital photography. The advent of digital photography nearly took down Kodak – one of the most blue-chip of blue-chip companies at one time.

In the early days of digital photography, the quality of the pictures was nowhere near what it has ultimately become. So Kodak didn't focus on digital, keeping its resources on selling film – for which it was so well-known.

Then the quality of digital images got better. Costs fell. When it became increasingly clear that digital was going to completely take over the market, Kodak had to scramble to get into the digital photography game.

Digital technology is a great example of something new that has completely transformed entire business categories.

But nowhere is disruptive innovation more evident than in the music business. Records and cassette tapes were replaced by compact discs, which are being replaced by MP3s.

Then there is music distribution: how and where people *buy* their music.

Conventional wisdom was that you had to go to a store to buy music – and the large music distribution companies liked it that way.

Then out of nowhere, HMV, Virgin, and all the other music retail chains woke up one morning to find that they had a serious new competitor to deal with: Apple.

Apple launched iTunes on April 28, 2003. As of January 2009, more than 6 billion songs had been downloaded, and online music is now the number-one distribution channel in the United States.

That's taking one idea (selling music) and another idea (electronic distribution of media over the Internet) and creating a new idea (online music sales). That's macro-creativity at its best.

Micro-Creativity

I encourage you and your organization to think about disruptive innovations, and how you can fundamentally change the nature of your business – for the benefit of your customers and society as a whole.

But not all creativity needs to be revolutionary.

Being creative doesn't always mean coming up with a million-dollar idea. Organizations can be improved through micro-creativity as well. There are all kinds of system improvements, process simplifications, or ways to increase knowledge-sharing that involve creativity and new ideas.

Like seeing the need for more internal communication on a project and suggesting a weekly six-minute conference call to keep everyone in the loop on what's happening. That's creativity.

Or moving the recycle bin away from some spot against the wall where no one uses it, to a spot next to the printer or photocopier where they will. That's creativity.

Or creating a simpler purchasing system or more efficient financial spreadsheet that's easier to use. That's creativity.

These are the little improvements that can be made every single day. Over time, they add up to a better, more efficient, and more exciting workplace.

The spirit of continuous improvement at Toyota demonstrates how small, incremental improvements, when taken together, can have a significant impact.

Strive to achieve big, game-changing thinking. But be proud of smaller improvements and creative ideas as well.

Don't Think You're Creative? You Are.

Preschoolers are creative. They use their imaginations every single day.

Painting a picture, building a LEGO tower, convening a gathering of superheroes, all require imagination. Kids picture what they want to do in their minds and then translate it into action. They do it naturally, often bringing other kids around them into their worlds as well.

We don't encourage creativity enough as adults, and especially not in the workplace. We are held back by fear – of failure, of ridicule, of being accused of wasting time.

This isn't just unfortunate, it limits the potential of our careers and the business success of our organizations.

Anyone who has changed the world, any idea that has shaped the upward movement of civilization, has used creative thinking.

Sometimes those creative ideas have not worked, but other times they have.

Unleash creativity in the people around you.

Help others to recognize how creative they can be.

Remember our simple formula: one existing idea, plus another existing idea, equals a new idea.

The result will be greater productivity, a corporate culture that helps you to stay ahead of the competition, and just maybe, a revolutionary idea that will make you famous.

Take Smart Risks

There are two kinds of risks: dumb risks and smart risks.

Let me show you what I mean.

It was a hot, beautiful, blue-skied afternoon in June.

Michelle, John, and I had gone to see Jackson's soccer practice. The practice had ended, and most of the kids and their parents stuck around to enjoy the great weather.

There was a splash pad and small playground next to the soccer field, and after running around during the hot practice, many of the kids went over to the splash pad and just got soaked.

Everyone was having a great time.

After splashing around awhile, some of the kids came back over to the playground, where there were swings, a climbing structure, and this old metal slide.

Keep in mind that the kids had just finished getting soaked, and some of them had gone sliding down the metal slide a few times. So the slide was wet.

That was when Jackson got an idea.

He thought that he could *surf* down the metal slide. Standing up, still wearing his soccer cleats – the kind with those plastic spikes on the bottom of the shoe.

Have you ever had one of those experiences when all of a sudden, the world starts going in slow motion? That was how Michelle and I witnessed what happened next.

We were over talking with some of the other parents, when out of the corner of our eyes, we saw Jackson taking up a surfer's pose at the top of the six-foot metal slide.

To his credit, he did make it down the first seven or eight inches or so of the slide. And then he fell right over, onto the hard ground below, breaking his left arm. All we needed to do was look at his forearm with our untrained eyes to see that it had a most unnatural bend to it.

Jackson was an absolute hero and trooper. Michelle and I were hysterical. Actually, it was mostly me who was hysterical – Michelle was cool and collected, if not calm.

It was not my finest hour when it comes to coolness and decorum.

We got to our car as fast as we could.

And sure enough, as I was pulling out of someone's driveway, trying to turn around, I came within a foot of getting into a car accident as we tried to rush to the nearest hospital.

Ultimately, Jackson recovered 100 percent.

But he learned a lesson the hard way on that hot June afternoon.

Surfing down a wet metal slide while wearing plastic soccer cleats, as we explained later on, was a dumb risk.

It is the kind of lesson that five-year-olds have been learning the hard way for quite some time, and forever it shall be thus.

But in other cases, people should know better than to take dumb risks.

A Very Costly Dumb Risk that Brought Down Barings Bank

Until 1995, Barings was the United Kingdom's oldest investment bank. It had helped finance the Louisiana Purchase. *The Queen herself* turned to Barings for investment counsel. Barings had survived the Great Depression, and two world wars.

But it was a few dumb risks taken by one single trader based in Singapore that would bring down this historic bank.

Nick Leeson worked out of Barings's Singapore office, and was making unauthorized trades that, unfortunately for him, lost money. This started to become a problem; not only was he not supposed to be making the trades he was making, but he was *losing* his bets. And he was hiding his losses in an account where others within the bank were unlikely to notice them – in what's called an error account.

To reverse his mounting losses, he made even *bigger* and *riskier* bets on rising Japanese stock prices. Leeson purchased thousands of contracts on the Nikkei 225, hoping that a big win would be enough to get him back to zero and clear his existing debts.

It didn't work.

On January 16, 1995, Leeson made yet another options trade. He had bet that there would be minimal volatility on the Nikkei – meaning that it would not move up or down significantly. The following day, a devastating earthquake hit Japan, sending the Nikkei index spiraling down – significantly.

And that, based on the actions of a single trader, was the end of Barings Bank.

Leeson's losses had reached more than $1 billion – twice the bank's available capital. Put differently, Barings didn't have the money it needed to cover Nick Leeson's bad debts.

Leeson abruptly fled Singapore, while the Barings officials in London saw their storied company collapse. After 232 years in operation, Barings was no more.

Leeson eventually went to prison, and Barings was sold to the Dutch-based financial giant ING for an embarrassing one British pound.

It's Still Good to Take Risks.
Just Take Smart Ones.

The problem that I see is that in efforts to reduce the incidence of dumb risks, organizations don't take *any* risks. The appropriate aversion to dumb risks gets carried too far, and people become reluctant to suggest or take risks *of any kind.*

Many managers have a tough time differentiating between smart risks and dumb ones. So they start rejecting new ideas and fresh thinking of *all* kinds.

What happens then is that people with new ideas make suggestions. And those ideas get shot down or criticized.

That's when creative, innovative people within organizations become reluctant to share new ideas, recommend new initiatives, or approach market opportunities in fresh ways. And over time, risk-averse cultures creep into existence. I wish I hadn't seen this happen as often as I have.

Taking smart risks is essential to the growth and success of organizations and of people's individual careers.

Smart risks are things like recommending an innovative new way of reaching out to your customers. Or developing a process improvement. Or trying something new that you think you might be good at doing.

Like the second time Jackson tried surfing. *Body* surfing.

We were on what the kids called our "beach vacation", when we went somewhere warm in the early springtime. And that's when Jackson saw a group of kids – not much older than he was – trying something that looked like fun.

They were riding the waves on boogie boards.

Jackson said, "I'd like to try that!"

So we went over to the guy in charge of kayaks, paddle boats, wind surfers, and yes, boogie boards, and asked if Jackson could give it a try.

At first, the guy in charge was a little reluctant because Jackson was only five. But when I explained that Jackson was a strong swimmer, and when Jackson himself said, *"Please,"* in as charming and endearing a way as he could, he got his chance.

He then spent the next hour or so riding the waves, learning about the ocean, and having an absolutely incredible time. That was a *smart* risk. Jackson wanted to try something he had never done before, something that pushed him just slightly out of his comfort zone, but that he felt that he could do safely and comfortably. Which he did.

Take Smart Risks. They Can Pay Off.

We all need to take more smart risks. But it isn't easy. Taking risks requires courage, confidence, and faith in oneself.

Take a chance on something in which you know you could be successful. Where you have the requisite skills and ability to deliver. Where you know that with a lot of hard work and the right attitude, you will overcome the inevitable obstacles and naysayers that will trip you up along the way.

Because only through taking smart risks will you grow, succeed, and make a meaningful difference as an individual, as part of a larger team, or in the world.

This is as important in our personal lives as it is in our jobs.

Take smart risks. Ask someone on a date, if you have a hunch that you really like them. Try getting out of the cycle of renting and make your way into the housing market as an owner. Go on a vacation somewhere new and different, somewhere you've never been before.

Try body surfing – like Jackson did.

Walk home on a different route than the one you're used to taking. Who knows what you might discover? Not down a dangerous street or in an unlit area – that would be a *dumb* risk! But you never know what great thing you might discover by trying something new.

Recommend a new idea. Follow a hunch and apply for that new role internally in a completely different department, but in a role where you feel in your gut you could make a massive contribution and change your career.

Have the courage to fight for what you know is right, even if it means challenging conventional wisdom – or one of your colleagues.

It's Hard to Make a Meaningful Difference in the Absence of Smart Risks

I often read the obituary page in the back of the paper, where they do a long write-up about someone who made a difference over the course of his or her life. These articles are reserved for people of achievement – who made the most of their time on this earth, and who did something truly meaningful.

I cannot think of a person, revered and applauded for good works at the end of a purposeful life, who hadn't taken smart risks along the way.

Take smart risks. It is the only way you can help change the world.

Take a Deep Breath and Use Words

"Take a deep breath and use words."

This is an actual expression that I heard a preschool teacher use when speaking with an irate and nearly hysterical two-year-old.

There is a lot of anger and emotion in a preschool. The toddler room at a preschool can be a particularly vicious place. The *Globe and Mail* newspaper once ran an article that described toddlers as the most violent people in the world.

Think about it. When they're angry or upset, toddlers bite. They push. They hit. They grab. They yell and scream. And then they cry, wail, and roll around on the floor. They are innately programmed to understand that resources – like milk or the blue car or the comfy red chair – are limited. And so their instincts kick in, absent *any* of the filters that we have learned through societal conditioning over the years.

Biting, pushing, and rolling around on the floor when someone doesn't get their way are behaviors that may not occur overtly in an office environment. But we've all seen people display the same kinds of behaviors, using more subtle and conniving means.

E-mails with double-entendres. Blocked progress on a project. Aggressive e-mails that are "cc'd" by someone to your boss, or your boss's boss. Or plain old uncooperative behavior.

Unfortunately, these actions are all too common – especially when promotions or bonuses are up for grabs. It all comes back to the scarce resources, either in the toddler room or in the boardroom.

Imagine if people didn't learn how to be subtle, discreet, and polite over the course of years of societal conditioning and training. What if people in workplace settings displayed the same kinds of behaviors as toddlers?

Picture this: Serious people in suits gathered around a boardroom for a meeting. Suddenly, and without warning, one VP presents a plan that would take money and clout away from another VP's department. This first VP, of course, had not told his colleague in advance that he would be presenting this plan. So the second VP feels a lot like a toddler whose toy just got snatched away.

What if instead of defending his department with words and arguments, imagine if the second VP handled the attack on his department like a toddler would: by leaning right over to the first VP, grabbing his arm, and biting him! I'd love to see the look on the faces of the other people around the table.

Toddlers are just starting to learn social norms and to develop filters for their behavior. Watching toddlers as they try to learn these subtle tricks can be very funny.

I remember being in the toddler room at preschool once, and seeing one boy pushing Jackson. Jackson, I'm sure, was not an innocent participant in this process; he had probably decided to "borrow" the other boy's toy or something along those lines.

In response to being pushed, Jackson got very angry, stepped forward, and yelled at the top of his lungs: "NO, THANK YOU!"

Not quite the diplomatic skills of Javier Perez de Cuellar (a Peruvian diplomat and former secretary-general of the United Nations) but it was a start.

The toddler room represents one end of the emotional intelligence continuum – where congenial discourse, respect for one's peers, and a sense of shared purpose may simply not exist.

But imagine what the *other* end of that continuum might be like – an enlightened, upbeat, supportive, self-actualized work environment. Imagine the high productivity of an organization where everyone adhered to a standard of discourse that was free from passive-aggressive behavior. Where people understood one another's personal perspectives, yet still focused on the organization's goals. A place where thoughtful discussions occurred about ideas, while leaving everyone feeling positive and upbeat and involved in the ultimate decisions made – even if it didn't go their way.

The times I have witnessed teams working at this level of enlightened interaction have been nearly intoxicating. These teams are like magnets: you just want to hang around them and join in the atmosphere of contribution, mutual support, and achievement.

There are many ways we can build work environments like this.

Talk to Each Other. Live and in Person.

One way to start building a more highly productive, positive internal culture is by changing our approach to e-mail.

There are parts of our brains that have learned over the millennia how to interpret the tone and emotional quality of a message. Those parts of our brains don't know how to interpret the tone of an e-mail. That's because our brains are reliant on non-verbal cues like the sound of a voice and facial expressions. So we often misinterpret the tone of an e-mail, get really mad, and start internal battles inadvertently.

How many of us have left the office at the end of the work day in a rage – an absolute rage – because of an e-mail that someone sent to us?

There are easy solutions for dealing with e-mails that drive you crazy.

If you get what you think might be a harsh e-mail, take a deep breath. Then use words by going to talk to the person who sent it – live and in person. Or if they are in another location, pick up the phone. That way, you can clarify what the real issue is and de-escalate the tension, rather than making it worse. And in some cases, you may find that you misinterpreted the tone and everything is fine.

One of the organizations with which we have worked has an "e-mail-free Wednesday" policy. I think that's a great idea – because it forces people to actually talk to each other. "E-mail-free Wednesdays" may not be easy to implement, but the spirit of using less e-mail is worth trying and should encourage people to get to know one another a bit better.

Be Self-Aware

While it is still best not to bite, push, or roll around on the floor, there are times when it *is* useful for us to be in touch with our inner toddler. Because sometimes things or people can make us *mad*.

As you can see from this picture, John was angry that afternoon. And he wasn't afraid to show it.

Kids are completely open about their feelings. As adults, many of us aren't nearly as good at articulating what's bothering us and addressing it in a calm, rational way that ultimately yields win-win scenarios.

Instead, too many people bottle up their frustrations, which leads to anxiety, upsetness, a lack of productivity and motivation, and in some cases, physical illness.

We live in a culture in which people keep their beliefs and emotions bottled up. The massage therapists, chiropractors, and drug companies love this. Because overly tense, stressed, and angry people who internalize their feelings are usually recurring customers.

How often has a work-related situation bothered you literally to the point where you feel ill and can't sleep? And what happens when you address the problem out loud, discussing it rationally, and ensuring that your point of view is being heard?

Incredible relief to yourself, and probably a better result for your organization as well. A bit more honesty and truthful articulation of what's really on your mind is healthy. Not biting or pushing or aggression of any kind – but honesty.

The big difference between the psychology of a two-year-old and the psychology of a member of your team is that the two-year-old is simply less subtle at hiding his or her true feelings. In my experience with two-year-olds, I have never found them to be subtle or ambiguous in their communications.

Kids *acknowledge* their emotions. We need to do the same thing.

So if something is really bothering you, write it down. Articulate it on paper. See how far you get. The act of writing things down might help you to identify a workable solution. You don't necessarily have to share what you wrote down with anyone else. But at the very least, writing your thoughts and feelings down should help you to reduce your level of anxiety and frustration.

Someone Acting Like a Jerk? Maybe They're Hungry, Tired, or Feeling Sick.

When our kids start getting really angry or cry a lot, it's a pretty safe bet that one of the following things is true:

- They are hungry;

- They are tired;

- They are feeling "off" somehow – either sick or needing to run off some excess energy; or,

- Something else is bothering them – like they feel that they were treated unfairly, or weren't getting the attention or recognition they think they deserved.

Once steps are taken to address whichever of these concerns was causing the upset, more often than not, we have a happy kid again.

What I find interesting, though, is that when I see *adults* acting like jerks, there is usually a root cause at play that isn't evident in the situation at hand.

Like the employee who is on some crazy diet, has a headache, and has a really harsh tone.

Or the co-worker with a newborn at home, who only slept for two and a half hours the night before and is snapping at you on the phone.

Or the executive who actually has some emotional challenges that he is working through, who goes completely berzerk in the middle of an important meeting.

Or the admin assistant who is going through a difficult break-up that is making her distracted and not a lot of fun to be around.

Remember all this when someone is being a jerk to you. It's quite possible that it has very little to do with you, or the work you're doing together.

A great question that my friend Rita Smith always likes to ask when someone is behaving strangely (or under-performing) is this: "Is everything okay?"

That's a brilliant question. Because it indirectly tells the other person that you're frustrated with their attitude or performance, but it also shows them that you're on their side – and not out to attack *them* as a person.

When you ask "Is everything okay" honestly and sincerely, you never know how the other person might respond.

Sometimes, things may *not* be okay, and they may have a serious health issue that they're dealing with. But even if that's not the case, chances are you will help them to identify what's really bothering them, and help them immensely.

So remember. When you feel like biting someone, take a deep breath and use words. Talk to them live and in person or on the phone. Not over e-mail.

If something is driving you crazy, take out a piece of paper and a pen and start articulating what you are thinking and feeling to get to the root of the problem.

And when someone is behaving completely inappropriately, they may just be hungry or tired or distracted. By asking them if everything is okay, you may earn their respect, confidence, and trust.

Take One Step Backward and Two Steps Forward

I love closure. When I think something is done, I like it when it *stays* done.

My quest for closure and forward momentum applies to business decisions, and to the completion of more mundane tasks as well.

Like building IKEA furniture.

When Michelle was pregnant with John, we made the trek out to IKEA to get some new furniture for his room – including a dresser.

We brought it home, and I opened the cardboard box and got to work. And so there I was, with all of the pieces of wood organized around the room, Allen key in hand, and instructions at the ready. If you've ever built IKEA furniture, you can picture the scene.

To their credit, IKEA designers do a great job with ensuring that their products are very simple to build. That's important for someone like me, because I am horrible with tools and completely lacking in talent when it comes to carpentry – even IKEA carpentry.

I remember when I was a kid in Cubs, my Cub Car was the worst – by far – in the whole Cub troop. To this day, I am terrible at building things with wood. If I ever had to give up management consulting to become a carpenter, my family might starve.

So there I was – the guy who loves closure and moving forward who is useless with work tools – building the IKEA dresser. Let me repeat: IKEA's instructions are clear and precise. Nonetheless, it seems that somewhere along the way, I skipped a step or attached something the wrong way.

I decided to carry on, hoping it wouldn't wind up being a big deal.

For about the next three steps, everything seemed okay. I was feeling good and hoping that the earlier mistake ultimately wouldn't be visible or really matter.

Next step: things were starting to look a bit funny, but no worries.

And of course – being a guy who loves closure, progress, and moving on – what do I do? I keep going.

But as of the *next* step, I recognized that the wood wasn't fitting as well as it should have been, and I was really starting to force things together.

The step after that is when the materiality of the earlier error became clear. That earlier error – now about six steps back – was suddenly a big problem. I could not, in good conscience, keep moving on without fixing the mistake I made before. Otherwise we would have had one heck of a poorly built piece of furniture on our hands.

So that's when I started going in reverse – undoing the work I had done, taking the time to go back and fix the problem.

I hate when that happens.

But it is absolutely the right thing to do. Because ultimately, it results in a better product.

In business, in the construction of IKEA furniture, and in life, it is against our nature to go backward. Or even to do something that *feels* like going backward when we've already invested a lot of time, energy, or money.

We crave progress. And it really bothers us if we have to undo things we've already completed when trying to complete any task. But if we remember what we are ultimately trying to achieve, usually the best course of action is to *undo* what we thought was finished. That way, we get a better ultimate result.

The United States Constitution: Starting Over to Get it Right

In the years following independence in 1776, America's Founding Fathers faced challenges and problems that were somewhat more complex than building IKEA furniture. They too had to go back and re-work something where they thought they had closure.

But in their case, it was a constitution.

America's early leaders and founders had come to recognize that their first constitution – the Articles of Confederation – wasn't working. The Articles of Confederation gave substantial powers to the states, at the expense of a strong national government. Every state had veto power, so it had become nearly impossible for the United States to be governed as a single jurisdiction. Congress lacked the power to tax, which made funding national projects difficult. And coordinating foreign policy was problematic, because northern and southern states had conflicting interests and objectives.

As a result, state delegates came together at a Constitutional Convention in Philadelphia in 1787, to take one step backward and two steps forward – and create a renewed United States Constitution.

It took rounds of negotiations, ongoing compromise, and lots of diplomacy to come to an agreement. Because of those early leaders' willingness to start over, the United States continues to be governed under the oldest written constitution of any sovereign nation in the world.

Where would the United States be today if the founders had not accepted the need to come together for the common good and rewrite the Constitution? Would an America governed under the Articles of Confederation have emerged from the Civil War united? Would it have enhanced civil rights? Put a man on the moon?

No one knows for sure. But we do know that the renewed constitution achieved all that and more, because the Founding Fathers were willing to take one step backward and two steps forward.

Breaking the Curse of the Bambino

The principle of making progress by going backward can apply to building IKEA furniture. And to the lawmakers of the late 1700s, coming together to rework the Constitution of the United States might have seemed like starting from scratch – but it delivered a better result.

The feeling of taking a step backward can also apply to letting go of star performers on a team as well.

At first it might feel like a big loss, but sometimes such moves can allow other key people to step up, unleash new energy, and result in better overall team chemistry.

For a decade, Nomar Garciaparra was the Boston Red Sox shortstop and a key player on their team. A fan favorite, Garciaparra could have been considered the cornerstone of the Red Sox future success.

In 2004, at age thirty-one, he was in the prime of his career. And that's when the Red Sox traded him – making room for other players.

For many Red Sox fans, trading Nomar Garciaparra could have seemed like a giant step backward. The whole baseball community was shocked at the news. Garciaparra had been traded to the Chicago Cubs.

After hearing about the trade, the New York Yankees' Derek Jeter said, "I can't really picture him playing anywhere else. You think Red Sox, Normar's the first name you think of."

Boston trading Nomar Garciaparra was a very counterintuitive move.

Over the years, Garciaparra had established himself as the kind of shortstop good teams need to win. But what happened from the trade deadline on Saturday, July 31 to the end of the 2004 season will forever be legendary in New England, and one of the best examples of taking one step backward and two steps forward you could imagine.

After Garciaparra left, the Red Sox started performing better. They made it to the post-season and all the way to the American League Championship Series to face their arch-nemesis, the New York Yankees – who are arguably the most successful baseball team in history, and one of the most successful sports franchises in the world.

If there was ever a test of the Red Sox management's decision to trade Garciaparra, it came against the Yankees.

And at first, it didn't look good for Boston.

The Yankees won the first three games, taking a seemingly insurmountable three-zero lead in the best-of-seven series. The Yankees only needed one more win to return to the World Series.

But Boston fought back. They refused to give up. The Red Sox were relentless in their determination to win. And they did – winning four games in a row, including Game Seven at Yankee Stadium.

Boston had done the unimaginable. They had advanced to the World Series, where they subsequently defeated the St. Louis Cardinals. For the first time in eighty-six years, the Red Sox had won the World Series – laying to rest the "Curse of the Bambino," from which the Red Sox had failed to win a World Series since Babe Ruth was traded from the Red Sox to the Yankees in 1919.

Baseball analysts and historians could endlessly debate whether or not the Red Sox would have won that World Series if Nomar Garciaparra had been with them. It's hard to say. But what we do know is that the Red Sox *did* win. And the lesson is that sometimes the removal of one individual from a team can unlock new energy. It can allow limited resources to be allocated differently, in a way that ultimately works better for the team overall.

The World Is Moving Too Fast to Not Challenge Sacred Cows

We can easily convince ourselves that something is essential to our success. That can be a person, or a product line, or a service, or the physical location of our business. We become fixated on the *essentialness* of things that might have been key to our success in the past, but might not be in the future.

Sometimes, moving out of a line of business or a program area can allow resources to be re-allocated in fresh and innovative ways. Freeing up those resources can ultimately yield far better results. But the initial psychological barrier of taking what seems to be a step *backward* is a difficult one. We become emotionally invested in things that we've worked hard on and built, and often stay committed to them longer than they are useful.

I suspect that many music distributors only wish they had pulled back from traditional retail stores and invested more of their resources building online distribution. Because all of a sudden, there was Apple with iTunes revolutionizing their business.

We live in a world of finite resources. The ways we choose to allocate our time, our money, and our mental energy need to reflect what will be most important tomorrow, not what mattered yesterday. And sometimes, that might mean moving away from projects, programs, or even people we've invested in for a long time.

So look around. Be willing to challenge sacred cows. Recognize that what might have worked well in the past might not deliver in the same way in the future. Given the speed of change in *any* market or industry, the ability to be flexible and nimble has become vital.

Wayne Gretzky once said, "A good hockey player plays where the puck is. A great hockey player plays where the puck is going to be." So determine where the puck is going to be.

Whatever your business might be, think about what success will look like five years from now, given your customers' needs, your competitors' strengths, and your own capabilities.

Then be willing to do whatever it takes to position yourself to be extremely successful in that future context – even if that means making decisions that might feel like a step backward today.

Get the Bad News Over with Quickly

In parenting and in life, we have to deliver bad news from time to time. News that will make someone feel bad, cause them anxiety, or in some cases, bruise their egos.

My wife Michelle and I periodically go out for dinner, or over to a friend's place for the evening. And often, one of my brothers comes over to look after the guys. This is a win for everyone: Michelle and I get some time on our own, my brothers get to play with their nephews for a few hours, and the kids get spoiled and allowed to do cool stuff.

In theory, anyway. Because there is always the "moment of departure."

On one such occasion, my brother David and his girlfriend Colleen came by to babysit. They arrived early so that we could show them where to find diapers, baby bottles, pajamas, and stories for reading before bed.

As we went through this routine, Michelle and I started to get a little anxious, because we knew the "moment of departure" was approaching. All parents dread this moment – the time when the kids are told "Mommy and Daddy are going out for a little while now."

Because from the kids' perspective, that's bad news.

Just as we were ready to leave, Michelle turned to Jackson and John and said in her nicest voice, "Mommy and Daddy are going out for a little while now." And John went ballistic. He lunged for Michelle and grabbed on to her ankles as he cried – with feeling and passion that would merit an Oscar nomination – "No, Mommy! Staaaaaay!"

He kicked. He screamed. He acted as an anchor, preventing Michelle from being able to move. This wailing and drama continued for about three and a half minutes. Think about that. Under the circumstances, three and a half minutes is an excruciatingly long period of time.

After much effort, we pried John off his mother, and David carried him away to allow us to put on our shoes and get out the door. The closer to the *finale* of our exit we got, the louder John became, and the more effort he put into stretching his arms out to Michelle.

The door closed. We made our way to the car, and drove all the way to the end of our street. And of course, in our haste to get out the door, we had forgotten something. We had left the address of the place we were going back at home. We drove back, and I cautiously approached the house to grab the little piece of paper with the address on it – and to check in on John.

Less than two minutes had gone by since we had left the first time. Stealthily, I opened the door to avoid detection. Within that short period of time, the wailing and extreme grief had given way to serene play. John was fine. In fact, he was playing cars with his uncle, showing David how he is supposed to push the little Hot Wheels cars around their track.

When we returned home later, Colleen told us that John stopped crying *within ten or fifteen seconds* of our departure. Once the bad news was over, he was fine.

If Bad News Is to Be Given, Move Quickly

Bad news isn't fun for anyone involved. But there are times when it has to be delivered. When that's the case, act quickly. Deliver the bad news professionally, with compassion, and then move on.

Michelle and I allowed the period of delivery of the bad news to last longer than it needed to. We let things drag on – which was hard on us, hard on John, and hard on others around us.

I am a firm believer that if tough decisions need to be made and bad news needs to be given, do it quickly and with as much class as possible.

That's true with personal relationships as well. When someone tells me they are in a difficult personal relationship, one that they've given a good try but that is just sucking the energy out of them, then my advice is very clear: end it. End it with respect for the other person and their feelings, but end it fast. Because ultimately, that's what is in everyone's best interests.

Don't Make it Worse on Yourself or Others

For most leaders I have worked with, there is nothing they hate more than having to let someone go. It is a gut-wrenching, painful, and horrifically unpleasant process for the person *doing the firing*.

Lawyers and human resources experts will tell you that there is a proper process to follow when letting go of an employee – one that reduces the legal risk to your organization and minimizes the overall unpleasantness. Seek their advice when you find yourself in that unfortunate position. However, as the person implementing the staffing decision, it is in your best interest – and your employee's best interest – to move quickly.

This Is Especially True for Organizations Going through Restructurings

Have you ever been within an organization where layoffs are pending? It is a truly awful experience. The anxiety level is suffocating. Speculation about who might stay and who might get fired is rampant. Productivity often plummets, and good employees begin to seek employment elsewhere.

If you are in one of those situations now, just know this: you're not alone in feeling as nervous and worried and frustrated as you do. In those situations where organizations are working through rounds of layoffs, the anxiety people feel from the potential threat of getting let go is often harder on many of them than when they are actually laid off.

So if you are in a position where you have to make tough choices, make them and make them quickly. Because then things can get back to normal and people will be able to get on with their lives.

Was John upset that night when Michelle and I were heading out for dinner? You bet he was. But the longer he was able to fixate on the problem, the worse it got. And then he was fine.

You will be too.

Pursue Your Passion

Now, everyone is unique in some way. Everyone has some aspect of their personality that is surprising to others, or that sets them apart. Some people have curious or obscure interests that last a lifetime, while others go through phases when they're really interested in something.

Like the time John decided that he wanted a death-metal biker tattoo.

We were on holiday one year, and Jackson and John wanted temporary tattoos. And the one John selected went right across his arm, featuring a black skull with flames coming out the back of it. Now, to be honest, a passion for death-metal seems somewhat counterintuitive based on what we know about some of John's other passions, which include:

- race cars
- race cars, and
- race cars.

Nevertheless, if John shows that he has a *passion* for death-metal biking and he shows some *talent and knowledge* in this area, I'd say bring it on.

Same with race cars. Here's why.

Winston Churchill Pursued His Passion. And He Changed History.

Long before Winston Churchill became a great orator and leader admired the world over, he was just a little kid. And Churchill had a favorite activity: playing with his toy soldiers. He would spend days playing with his soldiers, re-enacting historic battles.

Churchill's parents saw all this, and knew that Winston probably wasn't going to grow up to become an accountant or a doctor. And his parents *encouraged* him to pursue his passion.

Churchill's childhood passion for the military grew into a lifelong career. As a soldier, Churchill served in India, in the deserts of Egypt, and in the Boer War in South Africa. After returning home from active duty, Churchill took his passion for military strategy to a new battlefield – politics. As a Member of Parliament, Churchill would help shape British foreign and military policy.

These experiences helped prepare him for his greatest challenge: serving as British prime minister during World War II. Churchill's determination, his belief in the strong will of the British people, and his unwillingness to bend or break under extreme pressure, were an inspiration. Churchill inspired more than his fellow citizens and his armed forces – he inspired the world. His decisiveness and leadership guided British and Allied forces to defend Great Britain, liberate Europe, and win the Second World War.

Winston Churchill pursued his passion. And he changed history.

Feel Like Writing about Wizards?
It Just Might Work ...

As a young girl, she would read fantasy stories.

She had an active imagination and a talent for storytelling. From a very young age, she started writing stories of her own.

As she grew older, life was not always easy. Her mother passed away. Her marriage fell apart. She was a single mom, barely getting by, living on welfare, struggling with bouts of depression.

But during this time, throughout these setbacks, this young woman was following her passion: taking the ideas she had read about and imagined and writing them into a story. For five years, she juggled the demanding responsibilities of motherhood, while remaining focused and dedicated to finishing her book. It was about a young wizard who had special powers and abilities that made him different from his peers. His name was Harry Potter.

And her name was J.K. Rowling.

Rowling's passion for writing kept her anchored. As it turned out, she was good at it. Very good at it. And eventually, the discipline she showed in the pursuit of her passion would pay off. J.K. Rowling has become one of the wealthiest people in the United Kingdom, and has been credited by some for having re-introduced an entire generation to the importance of reading.

Pursue Your Interests and Passions

We're *all* a bit eccentric in our own ways. We all have quirks of our personalities.

But as we get older, we learn to conform, to fit into the clique, the team, the work setting. We lose our uniqueness because we fear that individuality, if not accepted by the group, will hurt our careers.

That's a shame. Because it is our individual personalities – and the different perspectives that they bring – that *strengthen* teams and organizations. Pursue your *own* interests and passions, and encourage your family, friends, and co-workers to do the same. Because we're lucky. We live in a time when there are countless ways that people can make a living from their personal interests.

Like traveling the world.

My friend and client Bruce Poon Tip is a visionary leader. His company, Gap Adventures, has revolutionized the world of adventure travel – offering people opportunities to travel to exotic locations around the world, including Antarctica. They even offer trips to the edge of space!

Gap Adventures is a leader in the travel adventure industry. Their success is, in part, a function of the internal culture and vibe that Bruce has created inside his company.

One of the organizational values that Bruce talks about with his team members is to *embrace the bizarre*. At first, I was a bit worried about this message, but then Bruce explained it to me. It is about *not being boring*. It is about leveraging the natural quirks, personalities, and talents of his people. The result is people who give their all and bring their passion, their quirks, and their creativity to work every day.

They are successful for a reason.

What are your natural strengths? And I don't mean what other people want your strengths to be. What are you just really talented at doing, compared to other people?

What is your passion? Listen to your hunches and find that sweet spot that combines the things you do really, really well and the things you love to do.

That combination of a real talent at something, and a genuine passion for doing it, very often leads to success.

Nurture and Identify the Talents in Others

Many people have difficulty recognizing their own talents. That's why leaders – including moms, dads, managers, teachers, mentors, and CEOs – should help others find their own personal strengths.

Many people are in the right organization but in the wrong job. Helping them uncover hidden talents can have an incredible impact on your organization, and on their careers.

Take Babe Ruth, for example.

Babe Ruth was an exceptional baseball player whose records lasted for decades. Many people still consider him to be the most purely talented batter of all time.

But before Babe Ruth became every pitcher's greatest challenge, he was a pitcher himself. His teammate, Harry Hooper, saw Ruth's potential as a hitter. Hooper suggested that he focus on batting. And the rest is history. By shifting to hitting instead of pitching, Babe Ruth uncovered where his true talent really was.

Follow Your Hunches

Let me tell you the story of Liam Scott, with whom I used to work.

When I first met him, Liam was working as an administrative assistant in a political office. He was very well liked, and highly regarded as a competent and upbeat guy. He supported the deputy chief of staff, and had a get-things-done attitude that made him popular around the office.

But Liam had a hunch. His gut kept telling him that he might be able to be a speechwriter. Turns out, he was right. He had the confidence to speak up, and he went for it – writing speeches on the side for members of the legislature.

I will always remember when we discovered Liam's hidden talent.

I was in my office, late in the afternoon, and a number of my colleagues had joined me. I had called them in because I was reading a work of art. It was one of Liam's early speeches, and even in one of his first attempts at serious speechwriting, his genius for finding the right idea to connect a speaker to his or her audience had shone through.

So there we were, gathered around, reading this great work. Then David Lindsay walked in. If you ever watched *The West Wing*, David was the Leo McGarry of our office. David was essentially everybody's boss.

I said: "Read this! It's brilliant." David only needed to read a few paragraphs to see what the rest of us had seen. He asked who had written it, and we told him.

"Liam? You mean Mitch Patten's assistant?" David asked.

Shortly thereafter, Liam wasn't an administrative assistant anymore.

In fact, he became one of the better speechwriters in the country. Liam's subsequent success has been far greater, and his career is far different than it would have been if he hadn't nurtured his own talent and pursued his passion.

Follow your hunches. Act on them. Liam did, and it has made a massive impact on his career.

There Will Be Challenges

I believe that everyone is a genius at something.

Your task: find what you're really good at doing, that you also genuinely enjoy or feel passionate about.

Because no matter what you do, there is drudgery.

There are dozens of clichés about how success only comes with hard work. I won't repeat them here. But never underestimate how much challenging, painful, dull, and difficult hard work there is in the pursuit of anything that is genuinely worthwhile.

There are parts of any job that aren't much fun. Just ask athletes or rock stars. They'll tell you – behind the scenes, there is a huge amount of work, unpleasantness, and pain.

Gold-medal-winning Olympians spend hours every day training. They religiously follow their diets without cheating. And they wake up early to practice.

Successful musicians spend months on the road, away from family, living out of the back of a bus.

But they keep at it. Because they've found their sweet spot – that rare opportunity that matches their inherent talent with something that they genuinely enjoy.

And more often than not, you don't have to look very far to get closer to that sweet spot. Look around within your own organization. Which department seems really interesting to you? Whose work do you get excited about? Which group is doing something for which you have always had a passion?

Five Ways to Discover Your Passion

For most of us, finding out what we're passionate about isn't easy. It doesn't come naturally. That's why we need to listen to our hunches, challenge ourselves to try new things, discover our passions, and uncover our own greatness.

So here are five simple questions you can ask yourself that may lead to clues about your true passion.

1. Think about the activities you liked doing the most in preschool, in middle school, and at the end of high school. What does that tell you about what you might like to do tomorrow?

2. What do you enjoy doing in your free time? Why is that?

3. When you catch yourself daydreaming, what are you thinking about?

4. Think about three people you admire. Ask yourself why you admire these people?

5. If you could only have one job in the world, what would it be?

Remember, you need to answer honestly. Genuine responses will help you to determine how you can lead a more productive and personally satisfying life.

Pursue your passion. And follow it to extreme and ridiculous lengths. You'll be amazed where it will take you.

The Shortest Distance Between Point A and Point B Isn't Always a Straight Line

It was a dark and stormy winter morning.

I was intense, focusing on a busy day ahead. And already, we were running behind schedule.

But my first task was this: get Jackson the toddler out of his diaper and pajamas, into his clothes, into a snowsuit, hat, gloves, and boots, and then into the car and safely to preschool.

So there I was – determined to achieve a precise goal. I was as focused on achieving it as Tommy Lee Jones's character in *The Fugitive* was on catching Harrison Ford's character.

I wanted the toddler dressed and into the car. No time for extra steps or consultation. That was my perspective on the situation.

Then, there was Jackson the toddler. Sitting on the floor in his pajamas, calmly playing with his plastic electronic toy that makes happy sounds. Jackson didn't see the urgency! He had no intention of letting me disrupt his zen.

So when I picked him up to take him over to the change table – even *with* his toy – he was displeased. He didn't want to get his clothes on, and didn't like my hurried and focused tone one single bit.

I wanted to get from point A to point B. And at that point, this meant getting his pajamas off and his clothes on – including his bright yellow socks.

So I got Jackson dressed, yellow socks and all, and brought him back downstairs. I felt well on the way to achieving my goal – getting Jackson dressed and in the car – when the phone rang. I put Jackson down and picked up the phone. It was an important client who was coming up to a pressing deadline. The conversation took all of fifty-nine seconds to complete. I then turned my attention back to Jackson.

In that short time, Jackson had successfully removed the yellow socks that I had worked hard to get onto him.

I thought that socks were off the to-do list. But now they were back *on* the to-do list.

And Jackson was very cross with me.

I was suddenly further away from the achievement of my real objective (get Jackson ready to go out the door and into the car) than before. I had made the mistake of focusing on the task (dress Jackson fast), instead of the achievement of my *real* objective (get Jackson quickly and safely to preschool). I hadn't thought about this problem strategically.

If I had taken a more strategic approach, I would have developed a vision and communicated it relentlessly! That vision would have been predicated on understanding my target audience (Jackson) and *his* objectives.

That might have included explaining to Jackson that in order to see his friends at preschool, he had to get dressed. That would have helped me to achieve his buy-in. Not only would he have kept the yellow socks on, but he might have been proactive and tried to get his snowpants on as well!

But by trying to move quickly – and skipping that step of explaining and communicating what we were doing – actually slowed me down, and pushed me one step *further away* from the achievement of my real objective.

Consultation and seeking buy-in may look like additional, time-wasting tasks as you work to get a project done and done fast. And taking the time for consultation and seeking buy-in certainly doesn't appear to be the shortest distance between point A and point B – which would be to just *implement,* without bothering to understand other people's perspectives.

But the shortest distance between point A and point B is rarely a straight line. Because in most large organizations (and even most small ones), you will meet with resistance, a lack of cooperation, grief, cost overruns, and ultimately, failed objectives if you don't build in time *and money* for consultation and buy-in.

Here's what I mean.

Say your objective is to get a new advertising campaign launched to increase your market share. Pushing to get the project done and done fast, you've got the rough cut of the radio ad in the can. But you didn't get the input or buy-in from the head of sales before going into the studio. Then, after having spent time and money on cutting the radio ad, you find out that the head of sales hates it. So back you go.

You may have stroked "cut radio ad" off of your "to do" list, but you're further *behind* in the achievement of your objective.

The best approach – for helping kids get dressed in the morning or getting your project approved and completed – is to allow time for communication and consultation, while helping everyone to remain focused on the vision and purpose of what it is you're ultimately trying to achieve.

Communicate the Ultimate Objective, Not the Task as You See It

There is an important lesson here for leaders. You have a choice: tell staff to do a task, or tell them to achieve an objective.

Say you are in sales. Your objective is to get a prospect to buy your product. You could ask your sales agent to call the prospect. That's a task. So your sales agent calls them, maybe leaving a terse and somewhat demanding message on a potential customer's answering machine. At that point, your sales agent thinks: *Mission accomplished!* He sees the task as off of his to-do list. And chances are, you are no closer to the achievement of your real objective – which is closing a sale.

Alternatively, you could communicate the ultimate objective to the sales agent, and say, "I think we could really help this prospective customer. Do you think you could find a way to match our offering to her needs?" That's an objective.

Perceiving his mission this way, the sales agent might call the prospect and suggest a time to get together and discuss how excited he is to learn more about her needs. He might then send her an enthusiastic e-mail with details about your new product or service. Now she's interested.

She is excited about how you can solve her problems, and she *begs* you to her office for a meeting at your earliest convenience.

Mission accomplished.

Don't mistake a task checked off of your to-do list with the achievement of your goal. Focus your attention – and your messages to people on your team – on the ultimate objective.

Celebrate Achievement

Little kids, especially preschoolers, celebrate almost everything. They celebrate birthdays. They celebrate the first snowfall of the year. They celebrate snack time. They celebrate using the toilet. And they celebrate seeing one another.

Rare is the day in a preschool when a great celebration isn't occurring. And we're not talking about major accomplishments. Our kids and their friends celebrate small wins and relatively insignificant successes.

We forget to do that sometimes, in our busy lives. We can learn from the preschoolers here. Because we need more celebrations.

Going Down the Big Kid Waterslide: That's an Accomplishment

At some waterparks, there is a height restriction that prevents shorter kids from going on some of the waterslides. This is the same challenge that many of us have encountered at Disney or some other theme park, where you have to be, say, forty-six inches tall.

When we went to one such waterpark, John discovered that he was indeed, at long last, tall enough to go on the big kid waterslide. So this got him very excited.

But then he looked up.

It was very high. And scary.

At first, he didn't want to go up. So we sat and watched some of the other kids coming down that big waterslide, some of whom weren't much bigger than John. Finally, after a few minutes, we asked him quietly, "Do you think you might want to give it a try?"

He nodded yes. And with a slow walking pace at first, but one that accelerated into a light jog as he saw other kids bouncing up the stairs for their next turns, John made his way to the bottom of that tall wooden staircase.

Slowly, he started climbing.

After what seemed like an eternity, he made it to the top, went down the waterslide, and splashed into the pool. And the look on his face when he stood up was as if he had just hit the home run that won the World Series.

He was celebrating this momentous accomplishment. And we celebrated right along with him.

Bring on the Celebrations

We need to celebrate more. And not wait for end-of-quarter success, or to provide well-deserved praise at a year-end performance evaluation. Celebrations need to happen in the moment. Right after someone does something really well. Employees should be recognized for their efforts. It's good for them and it's good for business.

Recognizing achievement is a great way for organizations to heighten engagement and increase productivity. As Daniel Kahneman, a psychology and public affairs professor at Princeton University, has said, "Business is more about emotions than most businesspeople care to admit."

A Gallup poll found that 82 percent of employees who receive praise or recognition are more motivated to perform better at work.

And that praise and recognition is *cheap*.

Many companies enjoy larger profits simply because their employees are happy to be at work. So this isn't about being nice and celebrating achievement for the fun of it. This is about beating the competition. It is about sustainable competitive advantage. It is about increasing the success of your organization – be that bottom-line profit, or another key measure that matters to you.

That's why celebrations and patting people on the back for a job well done matter: if people feel appreciated, they will work harder and stick with you, in good times and bad.

If Others Don't Celebrate Your Achievement, Do It On Your Own

Now, it may be that you know, deep down, that you just did a great job of something. But no one is organizing a parade with marching bands on your behalf. In fact, others *may not even have noticed* that you've done great work and done a great credit to your craft.

That happens a lot.

And that's when we all need to remember that while praise is great, it is personally knowing that we've worked hard and delivered a great result that truly matters most.

It is also important to remember the good things you *already* have in your life.

As Michael Bungay Stanier, the senior partner and founder of Box of Crayons says, "What's going well for you? The good things in our lives hide as ordinary, expected, unremarkable. So celebrate what's working now."

Michael is right.

We need more celebrations and recognition of great achievement, and we should all work to celebrate achievement within our own organizations. But let's also remember the importance of knowing in our gut when we've done something great. There are few more satisfying feelings than that personal sense of satisfaction that comes from having done a great job.

So recognize achievement – in others, and in your own work. And encourage others to do the same. Pat people on the back when they do a great job. Give a colleague a handwritten card when they go above and beyond, and tell them why you are proud of what they've done. Help to create a mindset of celebration and praise when praise is due.

Celebrating reminds us of the greatness in others … and in ourselves. The more we celebrate that greatness, the more of it there will be.

Get the Most Out of
Every Single Day

Ultimately, all of the lessons we learn from preschoolers are about how *we* choose to live. The stories are about *them*, but the principles and lessons apply to *us*.

More than just leadership and management lessons, the insights we get from watching preschoolers, being with them, and understanding them, apply to every single aspect of our lives: how we interact with others, how we lead, and how we form the basic philosophy that guides our actions and beliefs.

This section doesn't have a story about Jackson and John. It has a story about me. But it will shed some light on why it is that I believe some of the things I do.

Something's Wrong

As I think back upon it now, I knew that something was wrong because the echocardiogram technician was looking at the floor. She had just finished the test, and I had started sitting up. She was an Eastern European lady, about fifty, and she simply would not make eye contact with me.

She just kept looking at the floor.

In retrospect, it seems she tried to get out of the room where the echocardiogram testing is done as fast as she could – without seeming too obvious.

If you are ever going in for a medical test of any kind and the technician doesn't want to make eye contact with you at the end of the test, here's my bet: you have a problem.

And in my case, I did.

Lesson #1:
Go to the Doctor, Even If You Feel Fine

The spring of that year was a really exciting time. We had just learned that Michelle was pregnant with Jackson. We could not have been more excited, optimistic, and upbeat about our first baby and about our lives in general.

Michelle was making frequent trips to doctors, related to her pregnancy. And she got after me to have a physical as well – which I had not done for several years. Getting a physical was very low on my priority list. I felt fine, got a lot of exercise, and ate well. I was twenty-nine years old, and had no symptoms to report.

Finally, after increasingly assertive requests from Michelle that I just go to the doctor, I made an appointment at a family-medicine clinic affiliated with one of the big teaching hospitals downtown.

So I went. And the doctor assigned to me was great. She was still in medical school, doing her family medicine rotation. She asked me a number of questions, and I told her how everything was fine, that Michelle was going to have a baby, and that I felt completely healthy.

Then she went through the routine steps of the physical, and there seemed to be no issues. So everything was going along as expected, until the doctor got out her stethoscope. And after completing the listening procedure that they do, she paused and then asked, "Did you know you had a heart murmur?"

Now, I had heard of heart murmurs and was under the impression that lots of people have them. So I answered, "No, but that isn't a big deal, is it?"

"Well, it *could* be. So I'm going to send you for an echocardiogram test."

The discovery of my heart murmur by a twenty-something medical student on that day saved my life.

A week or so later, I went in for the echocardiogram, with the Eastern European technician who kept staring at the floor. I've already told you about what happened there. My follow-up appointment with the med student from the family-medicine clinic was a few weeks later. But in the meantime, I got a call from the assistant to a prominent cardiologist to set up an appointment to see him.

So I already had the Eastern European technician staring at the floor. A phone call to set up an appointment with a cardiologist? This was the second sign that something serious was up. Cardiologists are busy people. They don't usually call you in for an appointment just for the pleasure of your company, or to hang out. The fact that they were setting up an appointment for me to come in a few weeks later did not bode well.

Finally, I went back to see my med student at the family-medicine clinic to get the results from the echocardiogram. I already had two pieces of evidence that the news wasn't going to be good. As I was talking to the receptionist upon arriving at the clinic, I could see the doctor waiting behind the reception area. As soon as she saw me, she started staring at the floor.

I had now established a trend. When healthcare providers are privy to bad news about one of their patients, they stare at the floor a lot.

So the doctor escorted me to one of the examination rooms, where she broke the news. The heart murmur was caused by something called mitral valve prolapse. In my case, this basically meant that the valve between the left atrium and left ventricle wasn't closing properly, and much of the blood that the left ventricle was trying to push out was going back up into the left atrium. This is what cardiologists call regurgitation.

The mitral valve prolapse in and of itself wasn't the big problem. The problem was that in order to compensate for the prolapse, my left ventricle was working very, very hard. And like any hard-working muscle, it had grown very large. I suspect that this oversized left ventricle is what the echocardiogram technician had seen went I went in for the test – and she knew it was serious.

Over time, an enlarged left ventricle can cause a number of problems, potentially resulting in heart failure. That's different from a heart attack. Heart failure is when the heart reaches a point where it can no longer get blood to where it needs to go, including the brain.

At my follow-up meeting with the med student, she told me that based on her research, there were no drug-related means of correcting this. The only option was heart surgery.

She went on to say that she had referred me to a highly respected specialist who was best suited to take my case from there. That would be the aforementioned cardiologist, whose office had already called.

After that appointment, I took the subway back to work. I remember feeling a bit surreal – like I was in a parallel universe. Here were all these people going to work, to pick up their kids, to a movie, or who knows where.

And there I was with this crazy news that didn't seem quite real.

Because needing heart surgery is the kind of thing that happens to *other* people. You're always sad when you hear such news about others, and genuinely feel bad for them. But this kind of thing never happens to *you*.

And then it does.

In subsequent tests to determine just how bad my situation was, one doctor estimated that about 46 percent of the blood from my left ventricle was regurgitating back into the left atrium.

I met with the cardiologist, who was great. He didn't mince words, and he got the bad news over with quickly. He said that my situation was serious, and as the med student had told me, it required complicated surgery.

Then came the good news. He said that he was going to refer me to Dr. Tirone David, who was head of cardiovascular surgery at the University Health Network's Toronto General Hospital, and considered to be one of the greatest heart surgeons in the world. As it turned out, Dr. David had developed new and creative ways of repairing heart valves, which could fix my problem.

Dr. David is, in fact, a superhero. He doesn't wear a cape, but if you Google him, you'll see that he is considered a genius, even among other top surgeons. Dr. David's speed, skill, and innovations have saved, improved, or extended the lives of cardiac patients around the world.

The date of my heart surgery was October 28th. It was a complete success.

Jackson was born on December 1st – exactly thirty-four days later. And I was in the delivery room to be there with Michelle and Jackson.

I got lucky. Lucky that Michelle told me to go to the doctor. Lucky to have a great med student who found something wrong during a routine procedure examining someone who looked like a perfectly healthy patient in his twenties. Lucky to get a sharp cardiologist who was able to diagnose the severity and rareness of my case and know the right surgeon who could handle a complex and difficult case like mine. Lucky that I had a surgeon with a statistical track record of success that looks like an outlier on the far end of the charts. And today, I'm 100 percent healthy.

So go to the doctor. Especially younger guys, who notoriously don't get regular check-ups. Even if you are young and otherwise healthy, make an appointment and go to the doctor.

Because getting bad news and doing everything in your power to fix it is a lot better than the alternative.

Lesson #2:
If Life is Unfair, You Have the Right to Feel Sorry for Yourself. For Exactly Forty-Two Minutes.

Here's the part of the story I haven't told you yet. When I got home that day when I learned I needed heart surgery, I was really bummed out.

We all know intellectually that life can be hard and that bad things happen. But those bad things are supposed to happen to *other* people. Not *my* family! Not *me*! This was totally unfair. I had done nothing to deserve this, and there was nothing I could have done to prevent it.

It was the *unfairness* that made me the most frustrated of all. I felt very sorry for myself. And to some extent, that was normal, therapeutic, and necessary. But after a while, it becomes useless and unproductive.

So here's the deal. If life is unfair to you – because of a health issue, or getting laid off, or being passed over for a promotion, or getting dumped by your spouse or boyfriend or girlfriend, or having your reputation attacked unfairly – you have the right to feel sorry for yourself.

For exactly forty-two minutes.

Now usually, it's best not to use those forty-two minutes up all at once. Because when bad things happen – try as you might – you are going to feel sorry for yourself on more than one occasion. So my forty-two-minute rule holds. But just remember not to use up all of your minutes at the same time.

The day I learned I needed heart surgery was a bad day. But there were other days when I was frustrated as well. But you have to move on, roll up your sleeves, and focus on the future. Build a better tomorrow. And make the greatest contribution that you can with however much time you have left.

Lesson #3:
Get the Most out of Every Single Day

So here's the real message I want to leave with you.

You may not think that you're in a hurry to accomplish the things you want to do in your life. You may think that you have many years ahead to see the aurora borealis, or support a good cause that is important to you, or start a family. Let my story inspire in you a renewed sense of urgency.

Because you just never know how long you might have to get those things done.

So in the words of John Keating, the teacher played by Robin Williams in the film *Dead Poets Society,* "Carpe diem. Seize the day. Make your lives extraordinary."

Don't Forget to Enjoy the Ride

For thousands of years, philosophers have been trying to figure a lot of this stuff out. Some believe in just having as much of a good time as possible, while others believe that happiness comes from focus on work, achievement, and more tangible accomplishments.

It's a bit like the story of the grasshopper and the ant.

The grasshopper just wants to have a good time; enjoying the moment, but not planning for the future. But then, when winter arrives, the grasshopper doesn't have much fun anymore.

The ant works very hard; finding and storing rations, looking to the future, in anticipation of winter. The ant survives. He's got food to last through the winter, because of his discipline and hard work.

"The Grasshopper and the Ant" is oldthink. It presumes that you can *either* have fun *or* work hard to focus on the future to achieve things.

I believe you can do *both*.

And in fact, by doing things like following your hunches, taking smart risks, not being afraid to fail, playing games to make work fun, sharing, taking a deep breath and using words when you're angry, and ultimately, being a superhero, you can enjoy every day by doing great things every day.

This attitude applies equally to your professional life, your volunteer and extracurricular life, and your family life.

Don't be afraid to make your life extraordinary. Do great things for yourself, and for others, every single day.

So don't forget your cape. Be a superhero. Leave your mark. Find your passion by working to change the world for the better – in small ways and in bigger ones – every single day.

Bonus Chapter:
Jackson MacPhie Solves the Mystery of the Meaning of Life

So I'm putting the kids to bed. We've just had a great night but a late one, having eaten dinner at the home of a family we met through the kids.

My turn to help our guys get to sleep.

It was too late to read a book. So the lights are off, and Jackson asks if we can have what the guys call a "telling story," which is essentially a story that I make up.

I say no, because it is late. But instead, I tell Jackson that I have a question for him to think about as he goes to sleep.

So I say, "Jackson, instead of a telling story, I have a question for you to think about."

Jackson says, "What?"

And I ask, "What is the meaning of life?"

He hesitates for two-thirds of a second.

Jackson: "That's easy."

Me: "Oh yeah?!?"

Jackson: "It's about love ... actually I think."

Me: " ..." (no response).

Jackson: "Next question???"

I had none to ask, but I haven't stopped thinking about that since. It's about love, actually I think. Mystery solved.

Acknowledgments

I want to thank the many people whose selfless and generous contributions made this book possible.

Firstly, to the members of the MacPhie & Company team who worked hard to research, edit, plan, and – most of all – focus me on this book.

- Michael Genova – who breathed fresh life into this powerful idea, provided invaluable research and editing support, and brought an infectious enthusiasm to everyone involved with this project.

- Paul Tambeau – who demonstrated the difference between project management and project leadership.

- Karin Schnarr – who found the links between toddler behavior and doctoral-level management theory in record time.

Beyond the MacPhie & Company team members who contributed to this book, our friends and cheerleaders must also be thanked and acknowledged.

- Liam Scott for believing in this idea.

- Chris Dingman for acting as our private consultant on the nuances of change leadership and key performance indicators.

- Brett Laschinger for being a great ambassador for Clayton Christensen.

- John Toogood for helping me with my pronunciation.

- My friend and brother Laurence MacPhie for his wise advice.

- Jim Laird for his early inspiration and belief in this project, and for his in-depth tutorial about the life of a securities trader.

- Kiersten Eyes for being a great critic.

- Rita Smith for inviting me to contribute articles to her blog all those years ago, which helped form the genesis of the original "management lessons from your two-year-old" concept from which all of this grew.

- Rita Smith *again* for reviewing one of our early drafts and telling us that we were on to something.

- Joseph Lavoie and our friends from Navigator Limited for their insights into the Obama campaign.

- Michael Bungay Stanier for leading the way.

- David MacPhie and Colleen Stuart for steering us in the right direction and thinking big.

- John Duffy for thinking even bigger.

- And Lisa Geddes for teaching us that inspiration can be found everywhere.

The superheroes of this book are the members of my family. I thank them as well.

- My parents, Cathy and Robert MacPhie, who need not read this book, because they already live by its principles. They are a tremendous source of support to Jackson, John, Michelle, and me. This book is dedicated to them.

- Michelle, who rocks my world. Her calm but thoughtful counsel has immeasurably helped me through not only this effort but also the highs and lows that are inevitable in leading a firm like MacPhie & Company. Michelle, in her quiet but confident way, helps me deliver on the promise of who I could become.

- Jackson and John, who are my inspiration. I am so incredibly fortunate to have two cool, considerate, and thoughtful little friends to tuck in to bed each night. I love you guys.

Index

About the Author

Hugh D. MacPhie is a management consultant who advises corporate executives, leaders of not-for-profit organizations, and senior government officials. He is a principal with MacPhie & Company, a boutique management consulting, market research and communications firm. Hugh teaches popular courses on leadership, marketing, and communications, and shares the lessons from *Don't Forget Your Cape!* in an inspiring keynote presentation.

Hugh and his wife Michelle live in Toronto with Jackson, John, and their fish Goldy.

For more information about Hugh or to book him as a speaker, please visit *www.dontforgetyourcape.com.*